Sekhem Heka

Sekhem Heka

A Natural Healing and Self-Development System

Storm Constantine

Megalithica books

Stafford, England

Sekhem Heka
By Storm Constantine
First edition © 2008

The right of Storm Constantine to be identified as the author of this work has been asserted by her in accordance with the Copyright, Design and Patents Act, 1988.

Cover Art by Vincent Chong
Neteru, Shef and Aui illustrations by Olga Ulanova
Sekhem Heka Symbols by Storm Constantine
Temple illustrations by Andy Bigwood
Edited by H A Kiya Nicoll
Book Interior/Cover Design and Layout by Storm Constantine

MB0114
First edition by Megalithica Books, 2008

A Megalithica Books edition
An imprint of Immanion Press
http://www.immanion-press.com
info@immanion-press.com

Author's Web Site: http://www.stormconstantine.com

ISBN 978-1-905713-13-4

Immanion Press
8 Rowley Grove
Stafford ST17 9BJ
UK

Books by Storm Constantine

The Wraeththu Chronicles
*The Enchantments of Flesh and Spirit
*The Bewitchments of Love and Hate
*The Fulfilments of Fate and Desire
*The Wraeththu Chronicles (omnibus of trilogy)

The Artemis Cycle
The Monstrous Regiment
Aleph

*Hermetech
Burying the Shadow
Sign for the Sacred
Calenture
Thin Air

The Grigori Books
*Stalking Tender Prey
*Scenting Hallowed Blood
*Stealing Sacred Fire

Silverheart (with Michael Moorcock)

The Magravandias Chronicles:
Sea Dragon Heir
Crown of Silence
The Way of Light

The Wraeththu Histories:
*The Wraiths of Will and Pleasure
*The Shades of Time and Memory
*The Ghosts of Blood and Innocence

Wraeththu Mythos
*The Hienama
*Student of Kyme

Short Story Collections:
The Oracle Lips
The Thorn Boy and Other Dreams of Dark Desire
*Mythanima

Non-Fiction
Bast and Sekhmet: Eyes of Ra (with E Coquio)
Egyptian Birth Signs (with G Phillips)

*available as Immanion Press editions

Contents

Sekhem Heka: an Introduction
(Sek-kem Hek-aa)

In Ancient Egypt, *sekhem* literally meant 'power' or 'might'. The term applied to gods and goddesses and was often part of the titles of pharaohs and queens. The *sekhem* sceptre carried by rulers and important officials was a physical representation of their earthly power. In recent years, the word *sekhem* has been reinterpreted to mean the energy of a healing system named after it, but that meaning is of modern not ancient origin. Sekhem, in its modern sense, is a form of healing that derives from a system called Seichim, which itself is partly a derivative of Reiki.

Originally, the word *heka* meant 'magic' or 'magical power', and it was also the name of a god who presided over magic. This system of healing and self-development derives from my experience in the healing systems Reiki and Seichim and also in magical practices inspired by Ancient Egypt.

In formulating this system, I felt it was important that all the terms and names should have an Ancient Egyptian 'flavour'. The words I have chosen for many of the terms are not direct translations – and I do not claim to be an expert in Ancient Egyptian language! I used certain words that felt right, that matched the whole, and whose meaning fitted the requirements. The words take on meaning as they are used in a particular context.

I formulated the system for a number of reasons. Primarily, I have a great interest in the goddess Sekhmet and other Egyptian godforms, and have worked with their energy for many years. Once I became a Reiki Teacher, and discovered Seichim/Sekhem, I was pleased to discover that some Teachers had combined energy healing with Egyptian symbolism, and was keen to go down that path myself. Secondly, as Reiki initiation paves the way for self-development, I wanted to provide a system for my magical students whereby they could combine their studies.

What ultimately compelled me to produce this material in book form is the lack of printed information about Seichim and Sekhem in particular. Quite a lot of information is freely available on the internet, but somehow this has never translated across into printed form. Documents from the internet are useful, but I prefer to have a book in my hands, a physical artefact that can go in my library and be consulted when needed. There are many books on Reiki, and quite a lot on Egyptian magic, but I could find only a few that focused upon Seichim/Sekhem. I wondered why this was so, since the system appears to be fairly popular and there are some quite famous Seichim/Sekhem teachers out there who you might think would write books on their methods. It might be that some teachers have their own manuals, which they only give to their students. Or it could be that other teachers believe that a book isn't much use without the personal training, so what's the point of publishing one that isn't part of a formal course? But, if books are pointless in comparison to the personal education received from a Teacher, there would be no books on Reiki, and you only have to look in any book store or online book shop to see there are dozens of them.

A great many people don't wish to become involved in long public training courses or big groups. Or perhaps they live somewhere or have life circumstances that make it difficult for them to attend such events. Books such as this one help them get past that obstacle.

I've also written this book with the purpose in mind that

the system can be used by other Teachers for their own students. Therefore, I've included group practices and teaching methods, where appropriate.

You do not have to have received Reiki or Seichim attunements to be able to use most of the Sekhem Heka system. For those unfamiliar with the term, an attunement is a short procedure, performed by a Teacher who has taken the highest, often called Master, degree of an energy healing system. Attunements are the core of the majority of healing models based on Reiki and its derivatives, during which a person becomes enabled to channel universal life energy (chi or ki) through their body. Thus, the energy they utilise is not their own; it is universal energy channelled through them. It neither exhausts nor depletes you as you work with it.

Attunement has a tangible physical effect; the energy usually feels extremely and unnaturally hot – but not in all cases. Some practitioners experience the energy as very cold, again unnaturally so because the hands do not warm up during a treatment. Yet others simply experience the energy as a pronounced tingling in the hands.

An attunement can be a one to one spiritual ritual of some length between Teacher and student, or quite a short process, often performed upon groups of students at a time; it's all down to the individual Teacher's methods. The results, however, are the same. Any attunement set, performed by a Teacher (i.e. a person who has taken the highest degree), will enable you to channel the energy.

Note: Throughout this book, I'll refer to people who have taken the highest degree as Teachers rather than Masters. These practitioners are often called Masters after the Japanese style, but the Far Eastern meaning of this word does not have quite the same meaning as it does in the West. To me, Teacher is a more appropriate English term.

One difference between Sekhem Heka and Reiki is that Sekhem Heka can be used purely as a self and magical development tool, without the attunement process. There are parts of it designed specifically for previously attuned healers, but a lot of the material is suitable for those who haven't taken this training. I do hope, though, that after working with the system, non-healers are inspired to, or are intrigued enough, to get energy-healing training. This no longer has to be an expensive undertaking, and serious magical practitioners should not be put off by the 'New Age' tag. I've found Reiki and Seichim to be powerful complements to my magical work.

Anybody, whether they've been attuned to an energy healing system or not, can perform the meditations and rituals in this book and acquire the benefits from them. The fundamental point of any spiritual development system is (or should be) evolution of the individual. Everyone wants to feel as if they have power in their lives and are not just victims of chance fate. This is perhaps the most common reason anyone becomes interested in self development; to be in charge of their lives. To facilitate this, we can pick and choose the systems that suit our preferences or mind set at the time. Sekhem Heka has an Egyptian focus and veers towards magical ritual more than other systems of its kind.

The system does include attunement ceremonies, based upon the Reiki attunements in the way I received them. It's designed so that Reiki and Seichim Teachers can perform a self-attunement on themselves and then, after working through the system, proceed to attune others to the Sekhem Heka symbols. Anyone who has trained to Teacher degree level in one of the Reiki/Seichim systems can perform the Sekhem Heka Teacher attunement on themselves.

If you have not had Reiki (or similar) training you can work through the system without doing the attunements, although if you wish to, you could perform them as ritual exercises. Personally, I think it's preferable to have been attuned by a Reiki or Seichim Teacher first, so that you acquire the ability to channel the universal life energy most effectively.[1] But that is just my personal opinion. A few respected Reiki Teachers have claimed they were 'spontaneously attuned', and have never been initiated or attuned by another Teacher themselves. I have met individuals attuned by such Teachers, who channel Reiki as effectively as anyone whose Teacher derives from a lineage back to the Reiki founder, Mikao Usui. I have also met healers who channel energy through the hands, which feels exactly like Reiki to the recipient, who have never been attuned, and sometimes they've never even heard of Reiki. I do not discredit these claims, and am open to the idea that it is possible for spontaneous attunement to happen, or even that some people might be born with the ability. After all, it happened to Mikao Usui and Patrick Zeigler, the founders of Reiki and Seichim respectively. For this reason, I present this system in entirety, so that people, both with and without energy healing training, can experiment with all parts of it.

What Reiki/Seichim Is

To recap for the benefit of readers who are not already Reiki/Seichim practitioners: Reiki was the first system of this kind to find its way to the Western world. It is a natural healing system, which utilises, and in one sense actually 'is', the life-giving energy of the universe. Its name literally means 'boundless universal life force'. The word is used both as a noun and a verb, (i.e. you can 'reiki' someone), and it means the system itself as well as the energy used within it.

The system was developed by a Japanese man named Mikao Usui in the early part of the twentieth century, and eventually made its way to the West via an American Hawaiian, Mrs Hawayo Takata, who received Reiki treatment and subsequently became a student of it in Japan. Reiki has a long and colourful history, which can be read in many other books. There are a lot of myths surrounding its history, most of which have been debunked in recent years. A few of the best books, which I think are the most sensible, impartial and well researched, are listed in the bibliography.

In Reiki, (and its derivatives and comparables, such as Seichim, Sekhem and Karuna Ki), students are 'attuned' by a Teacher in an initiation ceremony. This procedure enables them to channel the universal life energy through their hands. From that moment on, the initiate is attuned to Reiki for life, and can 'turn it on' simply by asking, in their minds, for it to flow through them. Reiki works through intent.

At second degree Reiki, you learn three of the Reiki symbols that enable you to expand your Reiki practice. One of the symbols learned is the 'sending' symbol, which you use to 'send' Reiki over time and space. At third degree, you learn the master symbol, and how to attune others to the system.

Since it first became widely available in the Western world, around thirty years ago, Reiki has undergone many changes. After the death of Mrs Takata, who had more or less kept Reiki as a closed system, a lot of Reiki Teachers added to it, making it unique to themselves. It's a wonderfully versatile system, and does lend itself to being used creatively very well. Some Teachers have gone so far as to add new symbols and ritual techniques, while others see their practice as something essentially separate from Reiki – utilising a different kind of universal energy.

A lot of existing practices from other systems became included in Reiki teaching, such as the use of the chakra system – the energy network of the human body. In

Sekhem Heka, the focus is primarily upon the chakras. This was not part of Mikao Usui's original teachings, but the system does work well with Reiki and Seichim, and seems to fit naturally into their practice.

From information that came out from Japan, via the researches of such practitioners as Frank Arjava Petter and William Rand, it seems that Usui himself saw Reiki in terms of spiritual development rather than just a healing method. There is no doubt that attunement to Reiki can have a profound effect upon you, and precipitate a lot of changes in your life. It helps you to 'wake up' to reality, rather than to exist like a sleep-walker, unaware of who you really are and how you function. As 'ki' (or 'chi') flows through you, so it can help you become more aware, healthy and happy. Each time you give someone a treatment, you give one to yourself.

The Origins of Seichim/Sekhem

In 1980, an American named Patrick Zeigler underwent a spontaneous attunement while in Egypt. It occurred in the Great Pyramid of Giza, and was an experience similar to that of Mikao Usui when he first acquired the ability to channel Reiki, a long time before. Eventually, and some time later, after having taken Reiki training, Zeigler formulated a method to pass the energy on, perhaps having noted the similarities between Reiki and the energy he had experienced in Egypt. This system was first called Seichim. Because it had derived, geographically, from Egypt, from the very beginning it had Egyptian associations.

Over the years, as Reiki initiates learned how to work with Seichim, the two systems became fused, and now there are many crossovers between them, not least that Seichim attunement involves the use of Reiki symbols. (This is presumably because Patrick Zeigler used adapted Reiki attunements when formulating his initial Seichim system).

Although Seichim and Reiki are mostly regarded as separate systems, channelling different energy 'rays', I do not think the two can be separated, for the simple reason of the shared symbols. If Seichim attunements were performed without any recourse to Reiki methods, then that might not be the case, but they are, and this cannot be overlooked.

As with Reiki, many different branches of Seichim sprang up, and one of these was Sekhem. Although this was a term originally used by Patrick Zeigler, who has experimented with various different names for his system, it has been adopted by other Teachers, some of whom have greatly added to or changed the system. Sekhem, typically, incorporates the Egyptian goddess, Sekhmet, who was a ferocious lioness deity in ancient times, but who also had a healing aspect. Sekhmet's priests were also physicians, so it's easy to see how this goddess fits neatly into the Sekhem healing system.

Although the vast array of different Reiki, Seichim and Sekhem systems (not to mention all the other systems) might seem bewildering, as if there's just too much to learn if you want to pursue your studies, (and if you don't know where to look, then some of it does not come cheap), it's important to bear in mind that these systems all derived from individuals. These were Reiki, Sekhem, and Seichim Teachers who, through meditation, devised new symbols and perhaps underwent initiatory experiences. While the separate systems might have different 'feels' or 'flavours' for the practitioner, I do not believe they are entirely independent, or utilise completely different energy. Through my own experience, I believe it is down to perception and intention.

I have been initiated into Reiki, a number of derivatives

of Reiki, several forms of Seichim and another modality called Karuna Ki, but since then, I have experimented with the various systems and symbols. For example, during meditation, I've 'changed' the energy flowing though me from Reiki to Sekhem Heka to Karuna Ki, and it seems to me it's like turning up different colours on a TV set or monitor screen. What comes through might seem different to the perceptions, but it will still effect healing in the same way. I visualise Reiki as a pure white light, while Sekhem Heka changes colour according to what I'm using it for. Generally, Seichim/Sekhem energy is regarded as 'rainbow light'. If we apply it to chakras, some practitioners will say that Reiki is crown chakra centred, while Seichim and Karuna Ki are heart chakra centred. There are also subtle differences to how the energy is experienced within the body, but I'm sure everyone feels and sees all frequencies of the energy in different ways.

I connect with Sekhem Heka primarily for the purpose of self-development, to connect with the universe and to manifest results in my life. I connect with Reiki for healing and self-healing, and to send positive energy into situations and environments. Sometimes, the Sekhem Heka symbols will seem appropriate to use in a healing situation too.

The fact is that you can achieve all that you want or need to achieve with Reiki or Seichim, and everything else is just an interesting if often useful add on. I came to the conclusion that all the new systems that have sprung up since the initial versions merely concentrate on particular frequencies of the universal life energy. I do not think any of these systems are better or higher than the originals. They are interesting complements, formulated by creative Teachers. Neither are they lower or less effective, although it is interesting that none of the new systems (that I have come across) completely omit the Reiki symbols and attunement method. I understand that Patrick Zeigler's

SKHM system (yet another variation and I believe his current one) does omit the use of symbols, but I have not trained in that system myself.

It is my strong belief that any experienced practitioner can connect to Sekhem Heka, through regular meditation and openness to its manifestation. If you already regularly meditate or perform spiritual rituals, it should come easily. If you have taken Teacher degree Reiki or Seichim, the practices will undoubtedly feel more familiar to you, but to get positive results you simply need to want to experience them.

Sekhem Heka as a Complement to Reiki/Seichim Training

If you are already trained (or are currently training) in Reiki, I recommend you begin to work with the Sekhem Heka system after second degree. Some systems of Seichim incorporate Reiki training to second degree level, but Sekhem Heka does not. The reason for this is that I think Reiki itself should be learned in the form closest to its origins as possible. There is a danger of confusion and of cluttering the mind, if too much information is presented at once. Reiki itself is a beautifully simple and efficient system and I think its training should be a natural, relaxed procedure. There is so much you can do with Reiki, and I think that new systems should be introduced only once you feel ready in yourself to learn more. Also, Reiki derives from Japan, and has nothing at all to do with Ancient Egypt. Although I use the Reiki symbols as part of the attunement side of this system, I don't feel that Egyptian symbolism belongs in the basic teaching of Reiki. I recommend that people learn Reiki first, in its purest form, then branch out to continue their studies.

Those who are already attuned to Seichim can begin

working with this system as an extension of their current practice, since it derives from the same source. However, you would need to have received Teacher attunement to be able to pass attunements on to others.

Sekhem Heka as a Complement to Magical Practice

Sekhem Heka is designed for those interested in both energy healing and magic, so as to incorporate the channelling of the universal life force into ritual and meditation for the purpose of self-development, and also to affect positive changes in your reality. Any of the energy healing systems lend themselves to being incorporated into ritual, for those who wish to work with the energy in this way. The Sekhem Heka symbols act as foci on particular aspects of the energy. The deities – or neteru as they were called in ancient Egypt - can be visualised in a similar way.

I've read that some schools of Sekhem and Seichim claim that hands on healing was used by physician priests in Ancient Egypt. I did extensive research into this subject, while writing the book 'Bast and Sekhmet: Eyes of Ra' (Hale, 1999), and did not come across any evidence that the Egyptians used anything like Seichim in their healing practices. There is no doubt that the priests of the lioness-headed goddess, Sekhmet, were also regarded as healers, and neither is there any doubt that the priests used symbols (in the form of hieroglyphs) a lot in their practices, but there is no suggestion they channelled healing energy through the hands. That is not to say it did not exist – just that I did not find any evidence for it. In creating Sekhem Heka, I was not trying to emulate techniques that Ancient Egyptian priests might have used. This is a modern system that incorporates imagery, symbols and deities from ancient times. It is obviously influenced by the systems I have trained in, but like many other third degree practitioners, my creative side was eager to experiment and personalise.

While some practitioners like to believe in ancient origins for these healing systems, even to the extent of them deriving from mythical cultures like Atlantis and Lemuria, I prefer to think of Reiki and Seichim as modern systems, spiritually inspired by ancient practices and cultures and empowered by strong symbols invested with meaning.

If you already work magically with the Egyptian neteru, the material in this book will complement your practice, and perhaps bring another dimension to it. While the attunement side of the system does incorporate aspects of Reiki/Seichim, the rituals and meditations utilise symbols drawn from Ancient Egyptian hieroglyphs and can be used independently for ritual and meditational purposes.

The Use of Symbols

The process of acquiring symbols through meditation is part of what is called 'sacred geometry'. A lot of people who incorporate meditation into their Reiki/Seichim practices have received symbols in this way, which accounts for the vast array now included in the various systems. Symbols are foci that help you direct the energy towards a particular result. The symbols themselves are not the system: the energy is. But symbols are useful tools.

In the Usui Reiki system, there are four symbols: the power symbol, the emotional/mental healing symbol, the sending symbol and the master symbol. The power symbol can be seen as an amplifier of the energy. Visualising it in your mind, or drawing it in the air, 'turns up the power'. The emotional/mental healing symbol is used for exactly what it says, and often for helping to cure addictions. The sending symbol is for directing the energy to somewhere else, in space and/or time, from the practitioner's current location. The master symbol is used in third degree, when students learn how to perform attunements on others: it is also seen as a symbol of the highest spiritual light. Most systems I've come across incorporate a power symbol and a master symbol, albeit often in very different shapes. In the various schools of Seichim/Sekhem, you find much more specialised symbols, such as those that are used for work on past conditioning, inability to let go of harmful emotional attachments, planetary healing and so on.

There are symbols associated with Sekhem Heka, which you will work with as you study the different degrees, but you might find that you will acquire your own symbols to use as well. You might just 'see' a symbol during a meditation, or be inspired to draw one. This is a common part of working with an energy healing system.

The symbols in Sekhem Heka, as for any other system, each have a specific meaning and use. They are used as foci during meditations, rituals and healing sessions, to call upon that particular aspect of the energy. I have retained the use of the Reiki symbols in the initiation process, simply because, for me, they are the ones that work during attunement. Every system I learned after Reiki incorporated those symbols. I see no reason to change that, although it could be argued that any of the symbols are merely there to help us humans, as creatures of limited perception, to visualise, connect to and channel various aspects of the Reiki ray. Patrick Zeigler once said that the symbols are merely like 'training wheels', and that the individual practitioner should eventually dispense with the need for them. But at the moment, I feel most comfortable leaving the Reiki symbols in as part of the Sekhem Heka attunement process. Any Teachers experimenting with this system could try leaving them out and then observe the results.

The only symbol retained from other systems of

Seichim/Sekhem is the infinity symbol or lemniscate (the figure 8 on its side). This is because it was the original symbol used by Patrick Zeigler and therefore embodies the frequency of Seichim. Sekhem Heka is a derivative of that system, and it is this symbol, which is called Tcheru in Sekhem Heka, that unites it with its forebears.

The other symbols involved were inspired during meditation sessions with my friend and colleague Simon Beal, who helped me structure Sekhem Heka. From the outset, we felt that we should use different symbols rather than the ones already ascribed to different branches of Seichim/Sekhem. To us, it felt right that these symbols derived from an Egyptian source, so with that in mind we meditated upon the hieroglyphs to create symbols that best reflected what we wanted to achieve with the different degrees.

Shef
The Energy System of the Body

As with most other energy healing systems, Sekhem Heka works with the seven energy centres within the body, which in this system are referred to as the shef – the whole system – or shefats, the individual centres. These words derive from an Ancient Egyptian term that means power, energy, or vigour.

The energy centres are commonly known in most systems as the chakras, the idea of which derives from

Ancient India. The word chakra is from the Sanskrit, meaning 'wheel'. The centres are visualised as spheres or lotuses of coloured light, ranging through the spectrum from violet to red. The chakras can also neatly be applied to relate to various aspects of the human endocrine system.

In addition to the seven main energy centres, there are believed to be a great many additional and lesser centres within the body. All the centres are connected via energy channels known as 'nadis'. In Sekhem Heka, the focus is upon the main seven centres, which are positioned upon a central spinal column channel.

In the chakra model of human energy, the body is comprised of more than just a physical aspect. There are other energetic bodies that extend beyond the flesh. These are mainly referred to as the ethereal body, the astral body, the mental body and the spiritual body.

It's believed that if your energy centres are functioning properly – regarded as 'open' - then you function properly as a living being. The centres can become 'blocked' by negative emotion and experiences, which means that natural energy does not flow through the body freely as it should. This can give rise to illness, either physically or mentally, so you are no longer functioning at optimum level. Restoring balance to the shefats, opening them up again through meditation and healing, so that energy flows unimpeded, begins to repair the whole system: physically, emotionally and spiritually. Opening and enlivening the shefats is also believed to evolve the individual. For this reason, the idea of body energy centres is incorporated into many magical and healing systems, deriving from different cultures.

It's important to bear one fundamental thing in mind: everything that exists is comprised of energy. If we had the ability to see the microcosmic world, the buzzing atoms of the objects around us, we would see that the boundaries of things merge. It would be difficult to see where one object ended and another began. So in this way, everything is connected. A rock is energy, as is a human being, as is a thought or an emotion.

Negative thoughts and emotions have a detrimental effect on our selves, but unfortunately our way of life (for most of us) entails a lot of negativity. Half the time we might not even realise it, and think of ourselves as pretty positive creatures, but the legacies of our upbringing, our culture and its prevailing belief system can all play a part in stunting our growth. Part of learning to evolve as an individual is becoming aware of this negativity and working to change it. It's a life long process; those who believe in reincarnation might say it takes more than one lifetime. But if we can let go of the human desire to have things instantly, and look upon this growth as a graceful and slow natural process, we can let go of the stress of not being 'perfect' individuals after working on ourselves for only a short time. Don't strive impatiently for the destination of the journey, simply enjoy the journey itself.

The Correspondences of the Shefats

There are seven degrees in Sekhem Heka, and at each degree you will work with one of the seven shefats, beginning with Sen-t, the base shefat, which can be regarded as the seat of the animal self, survival fears, the fight or flee response. Qemhu, the crown shefat, is regarded as the 'highest', being connected with the higher self, spirituality and higher consciousness. Here is a brief overview of the shef.

The Base Shefat
Sen-t (ground, basis, foundation) (*sen*-tay)

This shefat is fiery red in colour and is situated at the base of the spine. Its element is earth and it is associated with the sense of smell. It also relates to the inner adrenal system that controls the 'fight or flight' response. Sen-t concerns survival fears, basic instincts, the animal self, personal stability, matters of security.

Sen-t's underlying principle is physical will, as opposed to the spiritual will embodied by the highest, seventh shefat of Qemhu.

When Sen-t is functioning correctly, you have a groundedness within you, a connection to the earth. You enjoy life, are stable, and feel secure – because you are secure within your inner being.

When Sen-t is dysfunctional, you can be filled with feelings of fear and uncertainty, or lack fortitude and stamina. In difficult situations, your way of coping is likely a tendency to flare up violently. Rage is used as a defence mechanism to shroud an underlying terror.

The Lower Stomach or Sacral Shefat
Khept-ti (male and female genital organs) (*kep*-tee)

Khep-ti is situated above Sen-t, below the navel and relates to the sexual organs. Its colour is a radiant orange, its element is water and it corresponds to the sense of taste. This centre is concerned with sexuality, sexual energy, desire, feelings, creativity, pleasure, self confidence, and general well-being.

This centre's fundamental principle is creative reproduction

– in all senses.

A healthy Khep-ti means that your interpersonal relationships are relaxed and fulfilling. You will be an open and welcoming kind of person, in all your relationships with others, platonic or otherwise. While creativity might find its outer expression via other shefats, it is born in Khep-ti, the seat of creation, both in terms of human reproduction and the ability to be creative in all aspects of life. An actively creative person will have an open and healthy Khep-ti.

When Khep-ti is blocked or dysfunctional, you are likely to be a cold and distant individual who finds it difficult to relate to others, especially in a physical or sexual sense. Emotions might be suppressed or denied. Quite often, problems in Khep-ti occur in youth, when sexuality first becomes active. A lack of physical bonding with parents can cause an inability to be physically close to others – even in the sense of being able to hug a friend or family member. It can also result in your outlook being narrow and rigid, lacking spontaneity and freedom.

The Solar Plexus Shefat
Hati (will, disposition) (haa-tee)

Hati is located below the rib cage and relates to the digestive system and the pancreas. It is the shefat of the sun, and it is thought that the body absorbs solar light through it. Therefore, it can be seen as your personal sun, the seat of your personal power. In colour it is a vibrant golden yellow, and its element is fire. It corresponds to the sense of sight and relates to will power, personal power, complex emotions, perseverance and determination. Here is born the ability to project the personality and affect your reality.

Hati's fundamental principle is the ability to shape reality and being.

The shefats can be split into several sections or classes: lower, middle and higher. Along with the heart and throat, the solar plexus centre forms the middle section. The desires and impulses of the lower shefats, Sen-t and Khepti, are purified and elevated by the energy of Hati.

An open Hati shefat means you radiate light and joy, which affect others around you. They will be drawn to that light. When Hati is functional, you will be tolerant and understanding of others, and completely comfortable with yourself. Also, if your higher chakras are open and whole, Hati is the first of the shefats to accommodate psychic awareness, in this case involving the sense of sight.

If Hati is closed and dysfunctional, a natural sense of leadership is perverted into the desire to manipulate and control. You will have a tendency to be restless and will need to keep yourself occupied constantly, in order to escape from the nagging feelings of inadequacy within.

The Heart Shefat
Ab (heart)

Ab is the centre of the body; three above, three below. It is located in the chest and relates to the thymus gland, which regulates the lymphatic system. Its colour is green, the colour of healing, and it relates to the element of air and the sense of touch.

Ab's underlying principles are unconditional giving and love; an elevated love that transcends all human insecurities and needs.

Ab relates to the ability to love unconditionally, compassion, wisdom, emotional stability, patience and tolerance, inner balance. It affords the ability to perceive beauty in the world around us. Ab is also the shefat of great healing.

When Ab is functional and open, you can truly have the ability to affect the world around you for the better. You will radiate natural warmth of being and sincerity. People will feel they can trust you. Just being near you can make people feel better. You instil hope.

But when Ab is dysfunctional you might have a tendency to attach strings to all that you give. None of your giving is without condition, so consequently you often end up disappointed and hurt. Or else the dysfunction can manifest as an inability to experience and give love freely, even to the extent of finding such things embarrassing and awkward. A closed Ab can make you a closed person, apparently friendly to all, but somehow distant and cold.

The Throat Shefat

Ashash-t (throat, gullet) (aah-*shash*-tay)

Ashash-t is situated in the throat and relates to the thyroid gland and metabolism. Its colour is blue and its element is ether. It relates to the sense of hearing.

The underlying principle of Ashash-t is communication; of ideas, thoughts, feelings. It is creativity and expression.

This centre relates to communication, sensitivity, creativity, expression, eloquence, and the ability to listen. As the last shefat between the lower and middle centres and the higher shefats of the third eye and crown, Ashash-t can be seen as a kind of bridge. The ideas and creative thoughts of the higher centres express themselves through Ashash-t.

Ashash-t enables us to reflect upon and analyse our thoughts and feelings. Through this, we can connect with our mental body and begin to differentiate between the different layers of our etheric selves. When functioning correctly, this shefat enables us to express ourselves creatively and clearly. Ether is an element seen as 'higher' than earth, air fire and water. But Ashash-t is as much about silence as it is about communication. It embodies the ability to listen to our inner voice, and in some ways to give ourselves a healthy distance from any immediate desires and needs so we can examine them objectively.

When Ashash-t is dysfunctional, the link of communication between your mind and body is blocked. You will be unable to reflect coherently on your thoughts and actions, and might be confused by unresolved feelings and conflicts, lacking the ability to analyse them. You might find it difficult to communicate – either by being shy and silent or else noisy and repetitive, unable to hold an audience. A truly blocked Ashash-t will result in a complete inability to express deeply held thoughts and feelings. The words would simply not be able to come out, held back and suppressed by a rigid throat.

The Third Eye Shefat
Aar-t (a goddess of the uraeus) (*aah*-tay)

Aar-t and Qemhu (the Crown) form the two highest centres of the energy body. Both can be said to be the seat of the 'third eye', but it is probably best to imagine them as a whole with regards to this function. Aar-t is situated in the middle of the forehead, above and between the eyes. It relates to the pituitary gland and extra-sensory perception. Its colour is indigo.

The underlying principle of Aar-t is self-awareness and self-knowledge.

This is the shefat of the third eye, awareness, perception, intuition, imagination, far sight and time. Aar-t is the seat of your higher mental faculties and your mental ability to affect reality.

For the majority of people, you have to have opened and enlivened all the previous shefats in order to have a fully functioning Aar-t centre. This blossoming is a natural result of working upon the shef gradually, up from Sen-t to Ashash-t. Once it begins to awake, you will experience heightened psychic awareness and intuition and will acquire the ability to see through reality, to be aware of the nature of the universe. Spirituality will feel natural and right, but at the same time you will appreciate the usefulness of logical thought and scientific analysis. A truly functional Aar-t gives us the mystical scientist – an individual who is curious about the workings of reality, and wants to explore them in an intellectual manner, but who at the same time appreciates the wondrous mystery of creation, and that which is beyond human perception.

When Aar-t is dysfunctional and blocked, this can manifest as being overly intellectual and devoid of any appreciation of spirituality, which will most likely be regarded as 'hokum'. You might be overly proud and vain of your intellect and consider yourself always to be right and those who disagree with you to be stupid. You will not be open to new ideas that challenge your ingrained beliefs, and can be aggressive in defending them. Your world view will probably be conventional and narrow, and the only reality that exists for you is that of the five physical senses. You will have no awareness of anything beyond that.

The Crown Shefat

Qemhu (crown of the head) (*Kem-*oo)

Qemhu is located in the centre of the head, although the shefat is often visualised as existing just above the crown, outside the body. Its colour is generally seen as violet, although it is also pure white light, the entire spectrum. It corresponds to the pineal gland.

This centre relates to the seat of your consciousness, the higher self. It is the shefat of empathy and true bliss through understanding. In Qemhu all the aspects of the lower shefats are united. It is their source of energy.

When Qemhu begins to open, you start to achieve true enlightenment. It's not likely to be 'blocked' as such, simply not active. An open Qemhu means awareness of your true self and a connectedness with the whole of creation. You will see yourself as part of the interconnected whole.

It is quite difficult to write about the consequences of an open Qemhu, simply because it is a personal journey for everyone. Neither is it an easy task to open it fully. It's not something you can work on only for a few weeks or months. It's a lifelong process of revelation, awareness and understanding. All of the work you put into enlivening and refining the lower shefats contributes towards this ultimate blossoming, an ongoing process of discovery.

Additional Shefats

As well as the seven major centres, most body energy systems incorporate multiple additional centres. In Sekhem Heka, the only other ones that might occasionally be significant or used are those in the palms of the hands and the soles of the feet.

The palms – Tchet-t (cher-tay)
The soles – Teb-ti (teb-tee)

The Tchet-t are stimulated during the attunement process, when symbols are placed into them.

When working with Sekhem Heka, the energy might be felt to emanate from the body from the Teb-ti shefats as well as from the hands.

End Notes:

1. If you wish to be attuned, it is not necessary to attend a Reiki/Seichim class and undertake a lengthy course. Nowadays, Reiki/Seichim Teachers offer attunements via the internet, either for free or a small fee. These involve what are called 'distance' attunements, whereby you arrange with your Teacher for the procedure to take place at a certain time. At this time, the Teacher will 'send' the attunement to you, when you should ideally be in a relaxed, open state, ready to receive it. While some years ago, many third degree practitioners scorned this method, more and more Teachers are now coming to believe that distance attunements are no less effective than receiving them in person – simply because the evidence is there in the satisfied students that they work just as well.

The Tiers of Sekhem Heka

All of the names for the degrees are taken or adapted from Ancient Egyptian words of appropriate meaning. For example Ha-a means 'first part', while Sen-nu means 'second time.'

Ha-a: the first degree
(ha-*aah*)

There are two neteru associated with this degree. The first is the lioness-headed neter Sekhmet, and the second is the neter of magic, Heka. The symbols introduced at this stage include Heka and Tcheru (*cheh*-roo), the infinity symbol. The Heka symbol equates to the Cho Ku Rei, or power symbol of Reiki that is learned at first degree. This is the glyph of the neter's name, as well as being part of the name of this system.

The shefat associated with this degree is Sen-t, situated at the base of the spine.

Sen-nu: the second degree
(*seh*-noo)

The neter of this degree is Isis. It involves the second shefat, Khep-ti, which is situated in the belly and associated with sexuality, desire, passion and creativity. The symbol for this degree is Tchem-Aset (*chem*-az-*ett*), the 'wings of Isis', which is representative of both creativity and protection.

Khemt-tu: the third degree
(*kem*-too)

The neter connected with this degree is Ra, the sun god. The third shefat, Hati, lies at the solar plexus, and is associated with will power and how we project our personality to the world. Khemt-tu also includes the five Sekhem Heka principles, which complement the Reiki Principles devised by Mikao Usui. Each principle involves a meditation, during which you examine aspects of your conditioning, the things that make you the person you are. The symbol for Khemt-tu is Aaten, the ancient symbol of the solar disk.

Ftu-Nu: the fourth degree.
(fuh-*too*-noo)

The fourth degree centres upon Ab, the heart shefat, connected with matters of emotion, unconditional/universal love and emotional expression. The neter for it is the cat-headed goddess, Bast, in her aspect of a goddess of love. The symbol is Per-Ahu (*pair*-a-*hoo*), which means 'the house of the heart'.

Tu Nut: the fifth degree
(*Too*-noot)

Maat, the neter associated with this degree, is the goddess of cosmic truth. The shefat of Tu-Nut is Ashash-t, the throat, which is connected with communication. The melding of Maat and Ashash-t promotes honest communication, with oneself and others. The symbol for Tu-Nut is Tchet-it (*chet*-it) meaning 'the spoken word'.

Sas Nu: the sixth degree
(*Saz*-noo)

The neter of Sas-Nu is Wadjet, the cobra goddess. Her symbol, the uraeus, is the serpent found on the crowns of Egyptian kings and queens. Wadjet as a serpent represents the third eye, the seat of intuition, clear sight and self awareness. The shefat Aar-t (aah-tay), found within the 'third eye' is connected with these qualities. The symbol for Sas-Nu is Ma-her (ma-*hur*), which represents a flash of light emanating from the Eye of Horus. This is because Wadjet, known also as Uatchit, is closely associated with the Eye, itself representative of inner sight.

Sefekh Nu: the seventh degree
(*sef*-ek-*noo*)

Nuit (*noo*-it), the neter of sky and stars, is representative of the path of magical seeking, as well as the higher self and knowledge. Sefekh-Nu is the 'Master Degree' of Sekhem Heka. Its shefat is Qemhu, the crown, which is connected with the idea of the higher, spiritual self. The master symbols of this degree are Tcher-Sekhem (*chair*-sek-*em*) and Aakhu (*aah*-koo), which are used for the passing on of attunement to this level.

Sekhem Heka Symbols

Detailed information about each symbol will be given within each level of the system, but here is an overview. All the words beginning with 'tch' are pronounced in exactly the same way as when expressing disapproval: 'tch!'

As in Seichim, the primary symbol of this system is the infinity symbol, the lemniscate, or figure 8 on its side. This symbol is used in rituals and attunements at all levels and in Sekhem Heka it is called tcheru (*cheh*-roo).

Sekhem Heka also utilises Egyptian hieroglyphs, pertinent to the system. The Utchat, (or Eye of Horus), and the Ankh, from second degree onwards, are drawn in the air prior to any ritual or meditation.

First Degree: Ha-a

Tcheru – limitless, boundless

This symbol is that of infinity, the double spiral. It represents the eternal and limitless nature of the universe and is representative of the Sekhem Heka energy.

Heka – magical power or energy

This symbol derives from the hieroglyph of the neter Heka's name. The outer 'box' represents arms reaching for the heavens, while the twisted shape in their embrace is said to represent a skein of flax. However, as Heka typically carries two intertwined serpents, the loops can also represent them.

Neter Symbol for Ha-a

Part of the hieroglyph for Sekhmet's name is a seated lioness goddess wearing the solar disk. This symbol is used to access the *heka* or magical energy of Sekhmet.

Second Degree: Sen-nu

Tchem-Aset – Wings of Isis

The name means roughly 'Wings of Isis'. In some branches of Seichim, there is a symbol called Angel Wings, but as angels are not parts of Ancient Egyptian belief, the protective wings of Isis, a recurrent motif in Egyptian religious art, seemed more appropriate. This symbol is used for protection, in whatever form, and also to help express and experience feeling.

Neter Symbol for Sen-nu

Part of the hieroglyph of the neter Isis's name represents a throne. She is sometimes shown wearing a crown in this shape. This symbol is used to access the *heka* or energy of Isis.

Third Degree: Khemt-tu

Aaten – the disk of the sun

This symbol is used for manifestation of desires, to seal magical workings and healings with Ra energy. It is also for transcending limitations and attaining full potential.

Neter Symbol for Khemt-tu

A hieroglyph that was used to represent the neter Ra is a solar disk bearing the uraeus, which is the serpent symbol often part of the crowns of pharaohs and neteru. It represents sovereignty and divine power and is used to access the *heka* or energy of Ra.

Fourth Degree: Ftu-nu

Per-Ahu – the House of the Heart

This symbol is used for healing the heart shefat and matters concerning emotion and emotional trauma. It is the ancient Egyptian symbol for a heart. The name Per-Ahu refers to the Hall of Osiris where hearts were judged. It meant the House of the Heart. Ab, the heart shefat, is the house of the heart.

Neter Symbol for Ftu-Nu

The perfume jar was a hieroglyph that formed part of the neter Bast's name. Perfume was sacred to her and an important part of her rites. This symbol is used to access the *heka* or energy of Bast.

Fifth Degree: Tu-Nut

Tchet-it – the spoken word

This symbol derives from two hieroglyphs – a staff, which means 'to speak' and two lips. The shefat of Tu-Nut is connected with communication. Blockages in this area can be caused by people biting back their words and expressiveness, keeping things bottled up. The symbol here is designed to help 'open up' this shefat so that communication flows freely.

Neter Symbol for Tu-Nut

In the halls of the underworld, the heart of a person was weighed against the feather of Maat, which represents truth, justice and purity. We can view the feather as symbolising honesty, open communication with oneself, others and the universe.

Sixth Degree: Sas-Nu

Ma-Her – the fiery flash of the Eye of Horus

This symbol represents insight, inner clarity and intuition. It is used to access the functions of the 'third eye' or Aar-t shefat.

Neter Symbol for Sas-Nu

The symbol of a hooded cobra is part of the hieroglyph for Wadjet's name. It is used to access the *heka* of this neter. The cobra represents wisdom, self awareness, imagination and clear sight.

Seventh Degree: Sefekh-Nu

Tcher-Sekhem (limitless power)

This symbol is a hieroglyph that means limitless power. It is the master symbol used to access the energy of Sekhem Heka for attunement purposes. Tcher-Sekhem represents the highest energy of the system – the equivalent of the 'great shining light' of the Usui master symbol Dai Ko Myo. It can also be used in healing sessions and to bring the full power of Sekhem Heka to magical work.

Aakhu

Aakhu literally means shining, but it also refers to a shining spirit and to words of power magic, and spells. The symbol here means 'to shine, rise of a luminary, being of light'. It can be used to access the higher self and for inner journeys to seek self knowledge. The light of the centre of creation rains down; from this place all knowledge can be sought.

Neter Symbol for Sefekh-Nu

This is the symbol for Nut's name in hieroglyphic form, and can be used to access the *heka* of this goddess.

Entering the Temple

Before embarking upon the path of Sekhem Heka, it's important to know about the symbolism and neteru associated with it. The beliefs of the Ancient Egyptians have been misunderstood and misinterpreted a great deal. It's not true that they worshipped idols of stone, or in fact that they had thousands of gods, although it might certainly appear that way at first glance.

The Names of the Divine

The Egyptians saw the divine principle as one force with many different names. It could be everything, everywhere, and all at the same time. The Egyptian word for a god or goddess was 'neter' or 'netjer', (plural: neteru), but the term also encompasses all the various representations of divinity. It can be seen as one divine being, with myriad different aspects, both male and female. It can be seen as the animating principle of the universe, the energy of the quantum realms. Because neter is one thing, an almost incomprehensibly huge idea, it can have immeasurable guises, immeasurable functions. It can be in countless places at the same time. It has no limits. Humans ascribe faces to different frequencies of this limitless energy – and these are the gods and goddesses who are familiar to us.

Heka: The Energy of Magic

The energy or power that the Egyptians believed caused effects upon reality was called *heka*. This was the force that the creator deity used to make the world. Each neter also had its own personal *heka* that can be seen as a personification of the neter.

Priests made offerings of food, drink and incense, and recited invocations to animate the statues of the gods and goddesses with *heka* of the relevant neter. Through the offerings, and a certain amount of flattery, they coerced the gods to enter the stone. In this way, an inanimate statue became a vessel of communication and a tool of magic. The priests did not have to visualise the neteru as pictures in their heads, but could focus upon them as living beings, resident in the carving before them.

In Egyptian mythology, *heka* was one of three creative powers that the sun god, Ra, used to bring about Creation. It is divine energy, literally the life source. The others are *hu*, which are Ra's divine utterances, and *sia*, his divine knowledge. *Heka* was also personified as a male neter, who was depicted standing in the boat of the sun to protect Ra, or else holding various ritual implements.

Although the word *heka* can be translated literally as 'magic', it's probably best to think of it in terms of: Life Force in Action. The priests used *heka* to connect with the neteru, and for maintaining cosmic order and balance. As a term, you can use it to denote all manner of supernatural powers and magical events as well as the energy behind them. It is the essence of the gods, life force itself. *Heka* is energy.

All neteru possessed *heka*, but the neter who was considered to have the most *heka* of all was the ibis-headed Thoth, who was credited with inventing both magic and writing and was the patron deity of scribes. Thoth's temple at Hermopolis possessed an acclaimed library of magical texts and ancient records.

The Egyptians had great respect for words and their inherent power. One of the titles of the goddess Isis is Weret-Hekau (*weh*-ret hekk-*ow*), which means 'great of magic'; a title applied also to Sekhmet and other goddesses.

The Egyptians believed that knowing a thing's, or a person's, name meant that you had power over it.

Heka was not regarded as possessed only by the neteru, since all living beings possess life force. People who were different from the majority in some way, such as dwarves, were believed to possess an abundance of *heka*.

Workers of magic also used *akhu*, which means 'magical power'. This word can also refer to a spirit of the dead, once they have passed through various transformation stages in the underworld. *Akhu* spirits were the most powerful and possessed great *heka*. But, in its magical sense, *akhu* can be regarded as the spells, enchantments and ritual acts required to access the *heka* of the gods. Both *heka* and *akhu* were seen as impartial powers that could be directed towards creative or destructive purposes.

The Neter Heka

The neter Heka did not have any temples dedicated to him that we know of, yet despite this he was an important part of the neteru because of his function. He was the son of the lioness goddess Menhit, who was associated with war, and the ram god, Khnum, who was a creator deity. With his parents, Heka formed the divine triad of Latopolis (Esna) in Upper Egypt. Another of Heka's functions was to protect Ra as he journeyed across the sky, making sure all hostile entities were kept far from the Sun God.

Heka was the patron of magicians and physicians, and the latter were often called 'Priests of Heka' and were believed to act under his influence. Doctor-priests would act as any modern physician in establishing the immediate cause of an illness or injury and prescribe the most effective treatment, but it was also their job to interpret the *ultimate* cause, which might well be the malevolence of a deity or spirit, or even a human enemy. Magic was then performed to deal with this ultimate cause.

Heka can be seen as the guiding spirit of Sekhem Heka. He embodies and personifies the living energy and is the 'contact' who enables results to manifest in reality. He carries two entwined serpents, which can be seen as symbolic of tcheru.

Keeping a Magical Record

Just about every magical system recommends that you keep a diary of your work. This is important, because we can so quickly forget details of dreams, rituals, meditations and healing sessions. Some people like to acquire visually attractive blank-paged books to write in, while others prefer to type up their experiences on a computer. Either method is fine. It's simply down to preference and what is most convenient.

Tools for Sekhem Heka

I have kept the use of tools to a minimum with this system. Usually, when I work with Egyptian magic, I have an altar and various other ritual paraphernalia to help psychologically create sacred space of the appropriate ambience. In Sekhem Heka, I see the energy itself as the only ritual tool you need. If you wish to have an altar, because it is part of your ritual practice and you prefer to, then by all means have one, but it is not essential.

The only tools I commonly use to practice Sekhem Heka are candle light, incense and music. These help set the mood and remove me from mundane reality. The choice of what music and incense are used is down to the individual. There is no right or wrong one that will enhance or obstruct the flow of Sekhem Heka.

The Prayers and Invocations of Sekhem Heka

The spoken parts of the workings have been drawn from different sources. Some derive from authentic Ancient Egyptian prayers and litanies, others are adapted from modern sources, and some I composed myself.

In particular, the invocations to Bast and Sekhmet are adapted from the work of Elizabeth St George, author of the two booklets 'Ancient and Modern Cat Worship' and 'Under Regulus: A Handbook of the Magic of Sekhmet'.

Ha-a
The First Degree

The first degree of Sekhem Heka introduces the concept of creatively mixing Reiki/Seichim/Sekhem training, healing and self-evolution techniques with magical ritual and Ancient Egyptian neteru.

The neter Heka is associated with all degrees of the system, but the neter that specifically applies to Ha-a is Sekhmet.

There are two symbols to work with during this degree; Tcheru (the infinity) and Heka. Heka is the 'power symbol' that is used to amplify the energy.

All the exercises in this system are designed to allow the individual to experience the energy and neteru as freely as possible, within a structured framework. If you wish to change or adapt any of the exercises to be more comfortable for you, or more inspiring, or more personal, then by all means do so. If new symbols come to you, work with them too. The instructions for the exercises can be regarded as guidelines only.

If you have already trained in a branch of Seichim, some of the exercises will no doubt be similar to ones you already perform as part of your practice.

For those who have had no training in energy healing certain of the exercises are designed to help you have some understanding and experience of channelling energy. It's not beyond the bounds of possibility that regular meditation might be enough for a spontaneous attunement to occur, so that physical effects are felt.

The Sen-t shefat is that which grounds us to the earth. If it is functioning properly we feel comfortable and at home in our physical skins, have plenty of energy and a sense of safety. When it is deficient, we can be overwhelmed by feelings of fear, constantly anxious and nervous, as if the world is just about to collapse on our heads. We mistrust others and have a poor relationship with the physical body.

Fears about money and security lie in this shefat, as well as any inability to visualise prosperity and manifest it, thereby becoming trapped in an impoverished state.

Restoring balance and vitality to Sen-t helps us reconnect with our bodies, promotes physical health and vitality and enables us to create prosperity in our lives.

Aui
The Hand Positions of Sekhem Heka
(aw-wee)

Most healing systems incorporate the use of mudras, which are hand positions or gestures seen as sacred and meaningful in Far Eastern and Asian belief systems. The most familiar mudra (*moo*-drah) is gassho (*gas*-oh), which means 'hands coming together'. It is the position people commonly use when in prayer. Mudras help aid concentration and are also useful for directing energy in certain situations.

During attunements, students generally sit with their hands in the gassho mudra. It is said that concentrating on the second fingers of the hands when in this position aids new practitioners to experience the flow of healing energy more easily. Many practitioners also use this position before healing or attuning others.

In Sekhem Heka, the hand positions are called Aui, (*aw*-wee), which means 'by my two hands'.

The 'prayer position' is called Tui, (*too*-wee) which means 'clean-handed' or 'purified'. It is used during meditation prior to opening the hands to send or beam energy, or before a healing to aid the practitioner to focus, and attain the desired state of mind.

To sit with the hands resting loosely on the thighs or knees, palms uppermost is called Au-ta (aw-taa). It derives from a word meaning to make an offering with open hands. Symbolically, it represents the way that healing energy channelled through you is returned to the world around you.

For the meditations in first degree, use either Tui or Au-ta, depending on what feels right to you at the time, unless the exercise mentions a specific position to use.

Meditation on the Tcheru

Tcheru can be visualised as the symbol that gives access to the energy of Sekhem Heka. It is the gateway. Meditation upon the infinity symbol is generally the first part of any Seichim/Sekhem system. It helps you connect with this frequency of the universal energy.

Compose yourself for meditation, in a soft lit environment, or outdoors if you prefer. Sit comfortably and rest your hands loosely upon your knees, thighs or lap, palms uppermost in the Au-ta position.

Clear the mind as best you can. Let thoughts and images drift by you. Focus on a blank 'inner screen'. Breathe deeply and evenly.

Now visualise the image of the Tcheru.

See it as slowly turning upon the blank screen of your mind's eye. It is a three dimensional object, not just a flat image. Visualise different colours of the spectrum pulsing through it. It might settle upon one particular colour for you, or not.

As you gaze inwardly upon it, think about how this symbol represents the frequency of Sekhem Heka. Ask for and intend that you connect with this energy

Visualise this energy streaming towards you from the centre of the universe. It might appear to you as a specific colour; just flow with whatever appears to you.

The energy is normally thought to enter the body through the crown shefat, but if it naturally flows into you through some other shefat, or even a different part of the body, again, don't attempt to change the instinctive visualisation – just go with it.

Relax and visualise yourself filling up with this warm, invigorating energy. Think about its healing aspect and how, as it fills you, it is healing you on all levels; physically, emotionally and spiritually. Visualise the symbol above your head, where the crown shefat is situated.

For some minutes, simply 'be' in the experience of the Sekhem Heka energy. Let go of negative feelings, worries, mundane concerns. Imagine that they are broken down, leaving your body through the hands, feet or breath, and that a more healthy energy comes to replace them. In the 'now' of this meditation, you have no earthly concerns. You are simply being yourself.

Channelling Sekhem Heka

Repeat the exercise above, only this time visualise that the Sekhem Heka energy enters your body through the crown shefat but centres in the heart shefat. Take your time with this. You might feel that your chest area grows warmer.

Visualise the energy filling your entire body, flowing into the place where your personal life force is said to reside: the area behind the belly. See the energy enlivening and enlarging your own, making it glow more brightly. (Again, this can be physically experienced as an increase in heat in this area.) Then see it expanding out through your entire body, down into your arms and legs. See yourself as a conduit; the energy enters you and you are able to direct it elsewhere.

Hold up your hands, palms outwards, and visualise the energy flowing from your own reservoir of energy, up through the body and out of your palms. Imagine the energy filling your environment, cleansing and nourishing it. And as it flows through you, so it enhances yourself.

Communing with Heka

In ancient times, Heka had no temples of his own. He embodied the energy of life itself. Gods and goddesses can be seen as masks we put upon the formless universal energy in order to interact with it. In this sense, they are separate from the concept of religion, which requires (usually) the act of worship towards a particular deity. In worshipping a divine being, praying for it to help you, you relinquish responsibility for your life.

The majority of magical systems encourage the student to take responsibility for themselves – something that is all too often lacking in modern life. It is our responsibility to work on ourselves, to become more aware and tolerant individuals, to become, in essence, better human beings. If we do something we realise was not the best way to react/behave/act, it is surely preferable to accept our mistake and learn how not to repeat it, rather than simply ask for divine forgiveness and think that's all we need to do for things to get fixed.

In Sekhem Heka you build up a 'relationship' with Heka, feeding him with your intention so that he becomes more 'real' for you. You can look upon it as personally recreating the idea of Heka for yourself as a magical tool. You can ask him to attend all of your meditations and healings as a spiritual guide.

Heka Meditation

Compose yourself for meditation in comfortable surroundings. With eyes closed, breathe deeply and evenly for a few minutes. Imagine the backdrop of your surroundings fading away into a mist. Visualise that you become merely a spark of consciousness within it.

Now, imagine that the mist begins to dissipate and you find yourself high amongst the stars, like a star yourself.

Amid this breath-taking beauty, connect with Sekhem Heka in your mind by visualising the Tcheru and asking for it to flow through you.

See the body of Heka form before you from motes of starlight. He is the energy of life taking on a physical shape, so that you can communicate with it more easily.

Spend some time meditating on Heka. Speak with him in your mind. Tell him of your magical intentions and ask for his company upon your journey.

Heka Empowerment

The power symbol is the hieroglyph for the neter Heka's name. It includes a shape that represents open arms and a spiral glyph, which can be seen as representing the two serpents carried by Heka. In Sekhem Heka, the serpents represent magic, wisdom and healing power. The shape incorporates the Tcheru and is also suggestive of the DNA spiral, the building block of life.

By visualising or drawing this symbol in the air you ask Sekhem Heka energy to flow strongly towards your intended destination/result. If you are attuned, you can use this in healing sessions as you would the power symbol for any other system you're trained in. If you are not attuned you can focus upon it as a channel through which your intentions are sent out into the universe. Every act of magical intention can be sealed with this symbol, locking the power of your desires into it. Obviously, attuned practitioners can use the symbol in this way also.

Heka Symbol Meditation for the Attuned

Compose yourself for meditation and connect with Sekhem Heka energy through the Tcheru.

Clear your mind and then visualise the Heka symbol shining before you. Spend some time gazing inwardly upon it, and see what ideas come to you concerning its use for you personally, or any personal meanings for it.

Place your hands upon your stomach for a self healing and keep visualising Heka. Intend to use it to develop you as an individual, to clear blockages and restraints caused by past conditioning, to help you redesign your life to bestow more happiness and satisfaction. This can be seen as a magical statement of intent.

Depending upon which system you have trained in, and how far you have progressed with it, you can experiment with using the Heka symbol in conjunction with the Usui sending symbol, or if you have not reached second degree, simply by connecting with the energy and using the symbol as you 'beam' it. (If you are unfamiliar with this term, it simply means holding up your hands with fingers splayed and letting the energy pour out of your palms into the environment.)

Heka Symbol Meditation for the Non-Attuned

Compose yourself for meditation and connect with Sekhem Heka energy through the Tcheru.

Clear your mind and then visualise the Heka symbol shining before you. Spend some time gazing inwardly upon it, and see what ideas come to you concerning its use for you personally, or any personal meanings for it.

Draw the symbol in the air before you and say its name three times. As you do so, intend this symbol to represent your commitment to self evolution.

Meditate for some minutes upon the sense of freedom you will achieve when you can free yourself of the restraints and blockages of past conditioning, fears and negative experiences. Focusing upon the Heka symbol will help you clear this 'unwanted baggage'. The arms of the symbol reach for the heavens. Visualise this as a process of opening up and letting go.

Communing with Sekhmet

Sekhmet can be seen as the ultimate self empowerment symbol. She is a fierce and protective neter, whose fearsome side is tempered by the fact she is also regarded as a great healer. She was the smiter of enemies, and if we can regard all our negative thoughts and emotions as our 'foes' then we can work with Sekhmet to smite them too.

Sekhmet was a favourite neter of powerful pharaohs. She was an Eye of Ra, an agent of the sun god, and would smite his enemies for him. At the time of year when the Nile ran low, before the annual inundation, disease was rife. The people believed that this was the time when Sekhmet stalked the land in her most terrifying aspect. Her 'Seven Slaughterers' were seen as responsible for causing the illnesses that affected people. But because she was thought to cause such terrible disease, the people reasoned she must also have the power to cure it. Thus, her healing aspect was created.

The Egyptian physician-priests worked to cure the 'ultimate cause' of an illness, rather than just the symptoms. Whereas they might have seen this as the effects of malicious magic or a spiteful ghost, we can view it nowadays as focusing upon evolving the mind, body and spirit, rather than just one aspect of ourselves. Heal the mind and spirit, and the body becomes healthier. It is an elegantly simple idea, and one long held in Eastern medicine. Nowadays, more and more Western medical practitioners are embracing this idea too. Through Sekhmet, we can work to heal the ultimate cause of our hurts and weaknesses, which essentially boils down to the sum of our past experiences and how they have affected us.

Desert Journey Visualisation

Compose yourself for meditation and clear your mind.

Visualise the backdrop of your mundane surroundings fading away into a grey mist. In your mind's eye, see the mist begin to break down and disperse, revealing a new landscape to you.

You find yourself in Ancient Khem, (Egypt), in what appears to be a lifeless desert. It is incredibly hot, unbearably so. All you can see around you is dunes of sand. You feel thirsty and tired. But you are here to seek your path and are determined to continue.

As you walk, you see a shimmer on the horizon, and black spots in the deep blue above it. You draw closer and see that these are birds. There is water ahead; an oasis.

You drag yourself to it wearily and find it to be a large, lush area. There is a pride of lions here, and other animals, but it is the lions that most attract your attention. They are drinking from the centre pool, and raise their heads as you approach. They offer no threat; they merely look at you and continue to drink.

You drink also of the refreshing water, and as you do so it fills you with renewed energy and strength. It is as if you are awaking from a deep and replenishing slumber. Now you are more than ready to continue.

Approach the lions and look for the one who will guide you. It leads you away from the oasis to a barren mountainous area that is silent but for the hiss of wind and the call of carrion birds. High cliffs rear all around you, dotted with dark entrances that might be tombs. It is an eerie, haunted place.

Ahead, you see an immense statue carved from the rock face, high up, reached by a tortuous narrow path. The statue is of pale weathered stone and is of the neter Sekhmet. It is almost invisible until you draw near, when it begins to 'materialise' from the stone before your eyes. Sekhmet gazes down into the valley, ageless and implacable. You can feel her power as you approach.

In the plinth of the statue is a dark doorway, which leads into the cliffs. Enter into this place. Within, deep inside the rocks, you come across a secret shrine to Sekhmet, where a black basalt statue of her resides. You direct the energy of Heka into the statue to summon her presence into it, so that you can commune with her.

Spend some time speaking with Sekhmet. Ask her to teach you.

When you re-emerge from the dark, incense shrouded depths of the shrine, gaze about yourself. Amongst the dry rocks you notice tough plants, lizards, and insects. Birds circle overhead. Realise that life is irrepressible; even in the worst conditions it is everywhere. It cannot be suppressed. Meditate upon this idea.

When you are ready, return to normal consciousness and open your eyes.

Sekhmet Temple

You can create for yourself an 'inner realm' temple for Sekhmet, where you can commune with her. The more you visualise this temple, the more 'real' it will become and you will be able to enter it whenever you wish.

As you did for the previous exercise, compose yourself for meditation and take your imagination into the inner realms. Visualise the place where the temple will stand; it can be of your choosing – a cliff top, a valley, deep underground. It does not have to be set geographically in Egypt, so you can use a fantasy world if you so wish.

If you want to, you can visualise the temple actually being built, either by your own hands or with helpers. Or you might visualise that the temple has always existed; you have simply rediscovered it. Try to imagine it in as much detail as you can; its rooms, shrines and gardens. There will be one room that is Sekhmet's domain, perhaps containing a statue of her. Lion imagery should prevail, and lions should also inhabit the temple complex. The colour red should also feature strongly. You can add to this temple at any time by repeating the meditation.

When you have finished building/imagining the temple, invite Sekhmet to take up residence. Part of the hieroglyph for her name is a lioness-headed seated woman, crowned with a solar disk bearing the uraeus (serpent symbol). You can use this symbol to represent Sekhmet and to summon her energy. Visualise Sekhmet entering the temple and spend some time speaking with her.

You can visit this temple whenever you wish to consult Sekhmet or speak with her, or simply to empower yourself when you're feeling weakened. Just by stepping across its threshold, the temple gives you strength: this is part of what you should build into it as you create it. You can also visualise this temple whenever you are performing the rituals of Ha-a.

Sen-t Work

Sen-t is the seat of the instinctive, animal parts of our being. It's where insecurities can cluster and block us. Survival fear can take many forms: it can be fear of others, fear of financial difficulties, fear of the world itself. Working upon Sen-t, using the energy of Sekhmet and Sekhem Heka to enliven the shefat, helps you control these often irrational fears.

It is useful to work upon sen-t if you should experience moments of panic and fear. Very few of us do not suffer from irrational doubts about our lives and security at some time or another. They do in fact have a function; they are called survival fears because they keep us alert to dangers. We could not do away with this function of sen-t, but neither should we allow ourselves to be overwhelmed by terror. A healthy sen-t is a sensitive animal 'nose' for what is and is not dangerous, and it is also a sense of being secure and safe.

The symbol of Heka, if visualised in the Sen-t shefat, can be seen as the foundation of the self, with the reaching arms of the symbol representing the self reaching for and connecting with the higher spheres.

Compose yourself for meditation and focus upon Sen-t. See its colour glowing vibrant red, and intend that the purpose of your meditation is to enliven and open it. Concentrate upon the positive aspects of the shefat – connectedness with the earth, a sense of belonging and security, groundedness, inner strength. See the colour of the shefat expanding outwards; vivid, strong and alive. Spin the shefat in a clockwise direction, all the time visualising it is becoming healthier and more open.

Sen-t Self Healing

This exercise is not only for self-healing but also for self-empowerment. You will take into yourself the fiery energy of Sekhmet that not only heals but purges. The idea is to purge yourself of negative thinking and lowered expectations of life. That isn't something you can achieve in only one session of meditation; it's an ongoing endeavour.

Compose yourself for meditation and connect with Sekhem Heka using the Tcheru and Heka symbols.

Go to your temple of Sekhmet and summon the goddess to you using her symbol. When she is before you, recite the following:

O lioness-headed one,
Turn your gentle face upon me.
O Great Sekhmet,
Cleanse my wounds within and without
Burn out all infections,
Burn out terror and fear,
O lion-headed goddess,
Grant to me your strength that I may be strong.
You dispel the fiends of sickness,
You vanquish plagues and despair,
You triumph, O Sekhmet!

Visualise that Sekhmet directs into you the healing ray of Sekhem Heka, burning from you all that holds you back, distresses you, hurts you, makes you ill. She commands the red frequency of the ray.

See this energy replenishing the energy of the sen-t shefat, so that it radiates a pure red colour. Feel this strength seeping through your entire being, so that you feel more vital and energised. If you stood up now, you would roar and feel ten feet tall!

When you are ready, return to normal reality and open your eyes.

Ha-a Initiation and Attunement

The initiation procedure in Sekhem Heka involves both a khesu and an attunement. Khesu means ritual or rite, and is used to describe such practices throughout this system. People who haven't been attuned to Reiki can also perform this khesu. In this case, omit the attunement part.

I have written this attunement with teachers in mind. A self-attunement is given in the appendices, which gives instructions for attuning yourself to the Teacher level of Sekhem Heka.

You can include your own magical/sacred space creating practices if you have them. This applies to all the attunement/initiation khesus in the system. The khesus can be as elaborate or as simple as you wish.

I have kept the visualisation fairly basic, so that you can add to it in your own words.

The student should sit comfortably with their hands in the Tui posture. You summon the shining light of Sekhem Heka, by drawing the Sekhem Heka Tcheru and Master symbol (Tcher-Sekhem) in the air and visualising the ray streaming down from the cosmos. Raise your hands above your head and then sweep them down. This gesture is to bring the light down to earth.

The following is the opening statement of intent. You can use my version or adapt it to your preference:

I call upon the mysterious ray of Sekhem Heka, in all of its power and brilliance. I call upon the adepts of the Ancient Egyptian mystery schools, to be present

here and bestow their blessings upon these proceedings. I call upon the gods and goddesses of Ancient Khem, and to any guides or guardians who have a connection with those here present, to join us now, and bestow their blessings, upon Ha-a, this first degree Sekhem Heka initiation.

Say to the student:

Visualise that you find yourself within a temple. There are tall pale columns all around you, and perfume burns in tall censers between them. The temple is lit by a myriad of small oil lamps on the ground. Walk through the columns now, until you come to a shrine at the far end. Here, there is an immense statue of the goddess Sekhmet. She holds an ankh in her hand.

We will now awaken the goddess.

Recite:

We call upon you, O Sekhmet,
O star of the lion's heart
Lady Of Transformations
Opener of Ways
Great One of Healing
Lady Of The Waters Of Life
We behold you in the heavens
O star of the lion's heart
Embolden our hearts, O Sekhmet
Embolden our souls, O flame, O lion star
Send forth your healing fire from the east
Kindle the flame
That is the essence of your healing power
And the heart of Sekhem-heka
Let the flame shine with your light

Send forth the ray of Sekhem-Heka
That we may look beyond the stars.
Shine upon our way
For we are true to you, O Star
Lady of Enchantments
Enlightener
Empowerer
Sparkling One
Great One Of Hekau
Sekhmet, Flame of the heavens.

Tell the student:

You see a brilliant light emerge from the ankh that Sekhmet holds, which indicates she has heard us.

Now perform the attunement.

There are many different attunement sets, and it would be impossible for me to give examples of all of them. What follows are guidelines. If the set you use appears to differ from the suggestions given below, simply adapt your usual procedure, but incorporate the two symbols Tcheru and Heka, and the Tcher-Sekhem Master symbol. If you wish, you could include the Sekhmet glyph, or else perform a separate attunement to Sekhmet. I've tried to keep the attunement part of this system as flexible as possible.

The procedure is the same as for Reiki attunements, except when you draw the symbols, include Tcher-Sekhem and Tcheru after Dai Ko Myo but before any other Usui symbols and Heka after all the other symbols. (A full version is given in the appendices.)

When attuning the crown, visualise that you push these symbols down into the brain stem along with the Usui ones.

When drawing the Cho Ku Rei on the palms of the hands, and 'slapping' them in, include Tcheru and Heka also.

After the attunement, resume the visualisation.

> Visualise Sekhmet coming towards you and the light of the ankh in her hand growing brighter. The essence of Sekhem-Heka is self-evolution and enlightenment.
> See the Tcheru come out of the light and enter your body.
> See the symbol Heka come out of the light and enter your body.
> Thank the goddess for the symbols, and spend a few moments communing with her. She may have important things to tell you or want to give you a symbolic gift.

After a few minutes, call the student back from their meditation and end the session. Affirm that the initiation is complete.

Khesu Ma-t

(khe-*soo mah*-tay)
A Rite of Sekhmet

Ma-t is a word for lioness and this khesu is designed to awake the lioness within. It can be performed after attunement as part of a Sekhem Heka training session, and regularly thereafter.

The words you will recite in this khesu are adapted from an Ancient Egyptian prayer to Sekhmet.

Visit Sekhmet in her temple. When she appears before you, visualise that she fills you with her power, so that you become one with her. You gaze upon the world through her eyes. With each breath you take, feel yourself growing stronger.

Say:

Behold, I smell the earth before the mighty one.
Behold, I am the child of Sekhmet, the lady of the east.
I am with her.
I am one with her.
I am the hand of the powerful goddess, wearer of the solar disc.
I am the twice beautiful one, more splendid than yesterday.
I am she who goes forth with Ra. I am she.
There is no part of me that is not of the goddess.
I am Sekhmet who comes forth in the dawn.
I am the power of Ra by day.
I shall not be dragged back by my arms and none

shall lay violent hands upon me.
For I am Sekhmet.
I am she who comes forth.
I am the seer of millions of years.
I am the power of the universe.
I dwell in the east.
I am the lady of eternity, the unveiled one,
My name is created to defy all evil.
I am the flame that shines in the sanctuary.
I am Sekhmet.

If you have a specific desire you wish to see manifest in reality, concentrate upon it, and direct the Sekhem Heka ray towards it, either with your mind or by sending the energy through your hands as you would for a Reiki sending. Believe that you can affect your reality in a positive way.

When you feel ready, conclude the khesu by stating, 'The work is done.'

Sekhem Heka Healing Session

If you regularly heal others, either casually or professionally, you might already work with the idea of balancing and enlivening the shefats of your recipients. In this case, you can simply adapt your usual practice to incorporate the Sekhem Heka symbols. But for those who are new the idea, here are some pointers for treatment.

You can acquire some sense of which areas need attention in your recipient's body by 'scanning'. This means putting your hands into the aura of the recipient a couple of inches away from the body. Move your hands up the body, from Sen-t to Qemhu, remaining alert for any discernible bumps, fizzings or cold spots you might feel in their energy field. You can also discuss with your recipient what areas they themselves feel need attention, i.e. in what areas of their lives they feel they lack control or effectiveness.

If you are working upon Sen-t, put the Heka symbol into your recipient's Sen-t shefat, either by visualising it, or drawing it in the air above that part of the body. Intend that this symbol clears the shefat and enlivens its energy, making your recipient stronger, more grounded and less of a victim of life's events.

Concentrate upon opening and expanding Sen-t. Visualise this as clearly as you can. You can ask your recipient to participate in the meditation side of the healing by concentrating upon their shefat too. Obviously, you can perform this healing on yourself as well.

For healing sessions with all the shefats, you can experiment with sending Sekhem Heka, using Hon Sha Ze She Non from the Usui Reiki symbols.

77

Sen-Nu
The Second Degree

Sen-nu means 'the second time'. The symbol for this degree is Tchem Aset, which means Wings of Isis (there is a similar symbol in other schools of Seichim known as Angel Wings). Isis is the neter associated with this degree, and the shefat is khep-ti, situated in the lower stomach. Khep-ti is connected to the sexual organs, sexuality, creativity and desire. Isis is a neter associated with love and sexuality, as well as being 'great of magic'. Isis can be a dark lady, but she is also a creature of lightness and humour. She has her reproductive aspect, as the mother of Horus.

Whereas Sekhmet and Sen-t have some dark and earthy aspects, Khep-ti is more concerned with general well being and the expression and fulfilment of desires. The creative urge springs from this shef-at, not just in the form of reproduction, but creativity on all levels.

If the Khep-ti shefat is deficient, it leads to an inflexible and rigid body posture, someone who is cold sexually and actually finds experiencing pleasure a problem. This usually stems from traumas in childhood, or having parents that did not show affection. The adult then has no idea how show or accept it. Such a type often creates a prison to protect themselves, which can come across as an impenetrable barrier to anyone trying to become close to them. Generally, they are unable to experience passion and excitement fully, and if such desires should strike they can retreat into themselves to escape. They also fear the inevitable changes in life, deal poorly with them.

An over-active Khep-ti results in people who can be

over-emotional, addicted to sex and who have a tendency to manipulate others emotionally to get their own way. Such is the great seducer who leaves a trail of broken hearts. Over-active Khep-tis can lead to hysterical mood swings, an inability to perceive when you are invading someone else's private space or a tendency to be emotionally clingy and obsessive.

If Khep-ti is healthy and functioning, we find warm, sensual people, very much in touch with their own feelings and desires. They might have a tendency to nurture and care for others and have no problems with their own sexuality, which they express freely.

The Aui of Sen-nu ~ Behut Aset
(beh-*hoot* Az-*ett*)

This hand position represents the throne of Isis and that is the meaning of its name.

Place hands in the Tui posture, then fold down the second, third and fourth fingers, and cross the thumbs. Only the index fingers remain upright.

Behut Aset can be used in either a horizontal or vertical position. Upright, you can use it in place of Tui for work involving the symbols and shefat of Sen-nu. The thumbs remain in a crossed position.

To use the position horizontally, uncross the thumbs. In this position Behut-Aset can be used to scan a person's body or auric field, or to direct Sekhem Heka energy into a desired place in its highest concentration.

Practice with both models of Behut Aset.

Sekhem Heka Sacred Space

You can create a Sekhem Heka temple using symbols and intention to enliven the environment with the appropriate energy. This is helpful before any magical work or to prepare a room prior to giving someone healing or an attunement.

The main symbols used for this purpose are the Ankh and the Utchat, the Eye of Horus. You should meditate upon these symbols before using them, so as to connect yourself with what they represent.

The Ankh

This symbol is that of life itself and is carried by many of the neteru. For ritual purposes, it can be seen as an affirmation of life. It can also be seen as meaning immortality and longevity – the persistence of life, if you like. In the creation of sacred space, it brings life to the temple. Visualise the Ankh as shining brilliantly with bright golden light.

The Utchat

The term 'Utchat' refers to either eye of the god Horus. The right eye is associated with Ra, the sun, and the left eye is associated with Thoth and the moon. In Sekhem Heka the left eye is used in the creation of ritual space. It symbolises magical power, wisdom and spiritual insight, qualities that it brings to your temple.

To prepare your space, first stand in the centre of area you wish to empower.
Raise your arms and connect with Sekhem Heka in your usual way. Visualise the light of its energy pouring down into you.

Now beam the energy out of your hands into the environment, intending that it clear the space of any psychic debris or negative energy.

Draw the Ankh and the Utchat before you, visualising them in golden light, calling upon the energy of what these symbols represent.

Say as you draw (or words of your own devising):

By the power of the sacred Ankh, this temple fills with the vigour of life.

By the power of the Utchat, this temple is illumined with the potential for wisdom and inner sight.

Visualise these symbols shimmering before you, filling the environment with their meaning and power.

Meditation on the Tchem-Aset Symbol

Tchem-Aset Meditation for the Attuned

Compose yourself for meditation and connect with Sekhem Heka energy through the Tcheru.

Clear your mind and then visualise the Tchem-Aset symbol shining before you. Spend some time gazing inwardly upon it, and see what ideas come to you concerning its use for you personally, or any personal meanings for it.

Place your hands upon your stomach for a self healing and keep visualising Tchem-Aset. There are several foci for this shefat and you might wish to concentrate on one at a time in separate meditation sessions.

Intend for Tchem-Aset to help you manifest your desires into reality and to enhance your creativity.

Focus also upon the element of this shefat that refines your interpersonal and sexual relationships. Visualise that your connection with others improves.

The wings of Isis also have a protective quality. The symbol can be used as a form of protection whenever needed.

You can experiment with using the Tchem-Aset symbol in conjunction with the Usui sending symbol, or if you have not reached second degree, simply by connecting with the energy and using the symbol as you 'beam' it

Tchem-Aset Meditation for the Non-Attuned

Compose yourself for meditation and connect with Sekhem Heka energy through the Tcheru.

Clear your mind and then visualise the Tchem-Aset symbol shining before you. Spend some time gazing inwardly upon it, and see what ideas come to you concerning its use for you personally, or any personal meanings for it.

Draw the symbol in the air before you and say its name three times. As you do so, intend this symbol to represent your creativity and desires manifesting in reality. Intend also that it is a symbol of protection whose power can be called upon at any time.

Meditate for some minutes upon manifesting your creativity and desires. Focusing upon the Tchem-Aset symbol will help you become more creative if you have been blocked.

Communing with Isis

Isis is a Hellenised version of the goddess's name, which came about after the Greeks conquered Egypt and sought to amalgamate the gods of that country into their own pantheon. Isis's Egyptian name is Aset, or Ast.

Isis had many temples dedicated to her in the ancient world, the best known of which is at Philae. The hieroglyph of her name depicted a throne, because she was thought to be intrinsic to the passing on of kingship to the pharaohs. She is always depicted as a regal woman, and wears upon her head various symbols, such as the throne, a crown of cow horns and/or the solar disk. Sometimes, she adopted an animal form, such as a white sow, when she was known as 'the Great White Sow of Heliopolis', and sometimes as a divine cow, in which form she gave birth to the sacred bull at Memphis. Because she could sometimes manifest as a bird of prey, a kite, she is often shown as having spreading wings.

Primarily, Isis is 'weret hekau', which means 'great in magic'. The myths surrounding her present her as a determinedly protective wife and mother, but she is also portrayed as intelligent, resourceful, uncompromising and occasionally fierce. She has knowledge of the underworld, as well as the celestial regions and the realm of earth, and is at home in any of these environments.

Philae Temple Visualisation

One of Isis's main temples in Ancient Egypt was at Philae, an island on the Nile in the south of Egypt. This temple was known as the Jewel of the Nile.

Compose yourself for meditation, and take your consciousness into the Inner realms. Visualise a new landscape appearing before your mind's eye: the Temple of Isis at Philae. You will visit it upon a festival night, when many people have gathered to celebrate together.

As you walk towards the main temple, gaze back to the banks of the Nile. Wherever you look, there is a blaze of light, as people have lit torches and lamps in the honour of Isis. Even the boats moored at wooden jetties bear brilliant lamps.

Enter into the main court of the temple.

Many people are present. They stand in silence and anticipation, and the only sound is the crackling of the torches they hold. The air smells strongly of lotus flowers.

Presently, female dancers and other officials of the temple melt out of the shadows of the columns. They wear the sacred lotus upon their brows and carry tassels of the papyrus plant. They are accompanied by musicians, who begin to play.

From the inner shrine comes forth a group of shaven-headed priests, dressed in white linen. They bear upon their shoulders the barque of Isis. The statue upon it is dressed in clean white linen, and the stone gleams because it has been anointed with scented oil. Flowers surround Isis, spilling over the edge of the barque, and you can feel her presence very strongly in the image before you.

Softly, the musicians of the temple sing praises to Isis, and the song is so beautiful it touches you deeply. Within its gentle cadences lie the mysteries of the goddess, her many aspects.

You lift your eyes to the sky and see, near the constellation of Orion, the bright star of Sopdet, the birthplace of Isis, known nowadays as Sirius. It is a radiant jewel in the heavens.

The priests carry the barque carefully to a boat moored waiting at the shore of the island. You see that many boats have gathered around Philae, so that Isis will be accompanied on her journey to nearby Bigeh, which is sacred to Osiris, her husband. Along with other celebrants you embark upon one of the boats, and presently the procession sets off along the Nile.

You see the island of Bigeh ahead of you, and it too is a blaze of light. On this night, Isis will be united with Osiris. The resting place of her husband is out of bounds to ordinary people, so everyone around you, apart from the boat carrying the priests, can only watch as the statue of the goddess is carried into the temple on the island. As they do this, people around you place small lights in papyrus leaves onto the water, so that the Nile itself becomes a river of light. Place your own light in the water, and in your mind make a wish, which you trust the goddess will grant to you.

When you are ready, return to normal consciousness and open your eyes.

Isis Temple

The hieroglyph for Isis's name is a seated woman, crowned with the symbol of a throne. In Sekhem Heka, you can call upon the *heka* of Isis by using the throne part of this hieroglyph.

Create an inner temple for Isis, and once it is created invite her to enter it. In order to keep the temple corresponding to Khep-ti, ensure that the colour orange features within it. Because Isis has many faces, it would be appropriate to include correspondences for some of her other aspects, if you are familiar with them. She has a mother goddess aspect, and is also regarded as 'great of magic'. She is the devoted sister/wife of Osiris, who in legend was able to outwit some of the most powerful neteru.

If you wish you can base your temple upon the Isis temple at Philaeby placing it on an island on the Nile, or you can invent one that is entirely personal to you.

All of the inner temples you create in Sekhem Heka are locations where you can commune with the neteru associated with each tier. The appearance of the temples *is* personal; they do not have to look like Ancient Egyptian temples if other images come to you instead.

When you are working upon the shefats, you can begin the work by taking yourself to the relevant temple in visualisation. It is down to the individual to be as creative as they wish with the components of this system. Therefore if you wish to devise rituals or meditations personal to you, using the imagery of the temples, neteru or the shefats, you're entirely free to do so. There are no limits placed upon the system or rigid instructions to follow.

Khep-ti Work

The second shefat is the seat of creativity and desire. If we look upon survival, found in the first shefat, as the fundamental drive behind the human psyche, then desire and the manifestation of desires is the second. The urge to create is an innate human quality, whether that is through acts of all forms of artistic expression including the ways we organise our lives, or the drive to reproduce the species. The wings of Tchem-Aset represent these aspects, and they also represent freedom. For once our desires are made manifest, this frees us. For example, if we find success through our creative endeavours in whatever occupation we have, it gives us the freedom to enjoy life more, whether that is through fulfilment of the self or release from financial worries.

Isis, as a symbol, encourages us not to compare ourselves with others continually, but to acknowledge our uniqueness. A lot of the time we sabotage all our intentions simply by thinking negative things such as 'miracles don't happen', 'why should I get all I want when I can see all around me that people are miserable', and so on. But if we constantly compare ourselves and our situations to others we unconsciously set traps of limitation for ourselves. Similarly, doubt can undermine our attempts to achieve the things we want. The minute doubt creeps in, it weakens resolve, intent and will. Isis tells us to reach for the stars, to walk among them in our minds, to stretch limits, to be creative in both our thinking and our actions.

Another important aspect of working on Khep-ti is learning to be focused. We can have many creative ideas bursting like fountains from our minds, but we need to build firm foundations for them, and work on them in a logical order, one at a time. Scattered energy does not manifest results as well as focused energy.

When working upon the shef, imagine that the different spheres and their symbols are like a totem pole, one above the other. Begin your meditations by visualising the Sent-t sphere and the symbol of Heka within it, its arms reaching up towards Khep-ti. Activate Sent-t by filling it with the energy of Sekhem Heka. See its colour grow brighter; it begins to spin in a clockwise direction, shooting off rays of brilliant red light. As this occurs it invigorates the shefat and opens it.

Now visualise Khep-ti, and place within it the symbol of Tchem Aset. Draw Sekhem Heka energy up from Sent-t to vitalise Khep-ti. See the colour grow brighter and the shefat begin to spin in a clockwise direction. It too benefits from this procedure, becoming more active and healthy.

See the two shefats as connected; the foundation of the self, with its basic survival instincts, reaching up for desire and creativity – that which separates humans from animals. The arms of Heka reach for the wings of Tchem-Aset.

Meditate for some minutes upon the qualities of Khep-ti and how they function within you and whether they need some attention. You can visit your inner temple of Isis and speak with her on these matters, ask for her guidance.

Sen-nu Initiation and Attunement

The student should sit comfortably with their hands in the Tui posture. You summon the shining light of Sekhem Heka, by drawing Tcheru, Tcher-Sekhem and Tchem Aset symbols in the air and visualising the ray streaming down from the cosmos. Raise your hands above your head and then sweep them down. This gesture is to bring the light down to earth.

The following is the opening statement of intent. You can use my version or adapt it to your preference:

I call upon the mysterious ray of Sekhem Heka, in all of its power and brilliance. I call upon the adepts of the Ancient Egyptian mystery schools, to be present here and bestow their blessings upon these proceedings. I call upon the gods and goddesses of Ancient Khem, and to any guides or guardians who have a connection with those here present, to join us now, and bestow their blessings, upon Sen-nu, this second degree Sekhem Heka initiation.

Say to the student:

Visualise that you find yourself in the courtyard to a temple. It is set upon an island in the Nile. The courtyard has a central pool and has been cultivated as a garden, with shady trees and fragrant flowers. Incense smoke drifts out from the temple buildings around you. In this garden stands a statue of Isis. She is shown as winged and kneeling, her arms outspread. Upon her head is the symbol of the throne.
We will now awaken the goddess.

Recite:

> We call upon you, O Isis,
> Weret Hekau, Great of Magic,
> Aid us in our spiritual journey.
> Open our minds, oh queen!
> Open our hearts, oh Ast!
> Open our inner eyes, oh beloved of Osiris!
> We come before you, in sight of Maat, in all honesty and integrity.
> Reward our work with your strength and wisdom.
> Teach us, oh Gold of the Gods!
> We will follow where you lead, oh Isis.

Tell the student:

> You see a brilliant light emerge from the statue of Isis, which indicates she has heard us. Her statue comes alive. She is a living, breathing woman before you.

Now perform the attunement.

As before, simply adapt your usual attunement procedure, but incorporate the symbols Tcher-Sekhem, Tcheru and Tchem-Aset. If you wish, you could include the Isis glyph, or else perform a separate attunement to Isis energy.

When attuning the crown, visualise that you push these symbols down into the brain stem along with the Usui ones.

When drawing the Cho Ku Rei on the palms of the hands, and 'slapping' them in, include Tcheru and Tchem Aset also.

After the attunement, resume the visualisation.

> Visualise Isis coming towards you. She is desire and manifestation of desires. She is all the ideas that can be imagined. She holds out her hands to you, and above them dances a star.
>
> See the Tchem-Aset symbol come out of the star and enter your body at the Khep-ti shefat.
>
> Thank the goddess for the symbol, and spend a few moments communing with her. She may have important things to tell you or want to give you a symbolic gift.

After a few minutes, call the student back from their meditation and end the session. Affirm that the initiation is complete.

Khesu Aset
A Rite of Isis

Create sacred space for yourself and call into you the energy of Sekhem Heka, using all of the symbols.

Now assume the position of Isis, kneeling, but with one knee raised so that the foot is flat upon the floor.

Raise your arms to shoulder height, palms outwards. Visualise that you have wings, spread out behind you.

Say:

> The sky is serene. Isis lives.
> She shines, a peaceful flame.
> I am a child of Isis, a child of light,
> As this Earth is a child of the Cosmos.
> I am a fount of creation, as Isis is,
> As are the neteru who have existed since the beginning of time.
> In the worlds above and in the worlds below
> They have been born as imperishable stars,
> Forever radiant.
> I am Isis, the star of Isis,
> I am one with her,
> And my Words shape reality.

Now concentrate upon the qualities you wish to bring out within yourself: confidence, the ability to be focused, improved relationships with others, the acceptance of desires, the ability to forge positive changes in your life through your own thinking and actions. Acknowledge that you and Isis are one.

Sen-nu Healing

Use the Tchem Aset symbol upon yourself and others in a healing session.

Begin by working on Sen-t, then position your hands over Khep-ti. Depending on the individual and what they need to focus upon in their lives, intend that the healing will either address sexual issues, help enable them to realise desires, or improve relationships with others. Intend for the symbol to open new roads for you or your recipient.

If you or a recipient should feel in need of protection, the Tchem-Aset symbol can be used during a session for this purpose also. Call upon the protective aspect of Isis.

Khemt-tu
The Third Degree

Khemt-tu means 'the third time' and the neter associated with this degree is Ra, the sun god. The solar plexus shefat, Hati, is the seat of our willpower, and concerns how we project our being to others. It is also connected with our powers of determination; in essence how much of an effect we have upon our world.

Our sense of self-esteem derives from this shefat and therefore how much confidence with deal with everyday life. If the shefat is deficient, you might be self-effacing and retiring, afraid to speak your mind or assert yourself. You might also lack energy. Khem-tu is the shefat of the sun and nourishing solar power. If the energy isn't flowing freely, it's like being in a permanent winter, when all seems drab and depressing. On the other hand, if this shefat is over-active, you could be the kind of person who is domineering and gets their own way through aggression and brow-beating others. Hunger for power, stubbornness and manipulativeness are also aspects of an over-active Khem-tu.

A balanced Khem-tu helps develop a responsible and reliable nature, someone who is able to lead fairly and inspirationally. Healthy self-esteem leads to a relaxed personality, who is able to discipline themselves when needed and whose general nature is warm and playful.

This degree also includes the Sekhem Heka principles, which are designed to complement the Usui principles of Reiki.

The Aui of Khemt-tu - Temati
(tem-ah-tee)

The Aui of this degree is called Temati, which means 'a pair of wings'. The arms are held out straight at shoulder height. In Sen-nu, you used a similar position while kneeling during the Isis khesu. In Khemt-tu, you will use the aui when standing upright.

Temati can be used when making statements of intent at the beginning of khesus, healing sessions or attunement ceremonies. It can be used when calling upon the neteru.

Stand within your sacred space with your arms in this position. See the Tcheru shining above your crown shefat. Draw the light of Sekhem Heka down into your being. Visualise that it radiates through your body, down your arms and out of your hands. In this position you are a shining star of universal energy. Beam this energy out into the environment.

Meditation on the Aaten Symbol

Aaten Meditation for the Attuned

Compose yourself for meditation and connect with Sekhem Heka energy through the Tcheru.

Clear your mind and then visualise the Aaten symbol shining before you. Spend some time gazing inwardly upon it, and see what ideas come to you concerning its use for you personally, or any personal meanings for it.

Place your hands upon your solar plexus for a self healing and keep visualising Aaten. Use it to help focus your willpower, to call upon your inner strength and enable you to project your will more effectively to accomplish objectives. Imagine that the pure golden radiance of this symbol fills your being. You can direct it towards a specific purpose and say 'I will this to be so!' The Aaten is almost like a magical exclamation mark! It seals your will and your intention into a desired result.

Experiment with using the Aaten symbol in conjunction with the Usui sending symbol, or if you have not reached second degree, simply by connecting with the energy and using the symbol as you 'beam' it.

Aaten Meditation for the Non-Attuned

Compose yourself for meditation and connect with Sekhem Heka energy through the Tcheru.

Clear your mind and then visualise the Aaten symbol shining before you. Spend some time gazing inwardly upon it, and see what ideas come to you concerning its use for you personally, or any personal meanings for it.

Draw the symbol in the air before you and say its name three times. As you do so, intend this symbol to represent your will and your ability to project your intentions to accomplish positive results.

Meditate for some minutes upon having the confidence and certainty to project your will to achieve all your aims.

Communing with Ra

Ra, sometimes spelled Re, was an Egyptian creator god specifically connected with the sun and its daily journey across the heavens. The sun rising above the horizon each morning was regarded as the ultimate symbol of creation. Its travels across the sky, from morning to night, were regarded as symbolic of the whole cycle of life: birth, life, death and rebirth.

 Ra can be shown with either the head of a hawk or of a ram, but his image is also that of the sun itself. One of the hieroglyphs used to represent him is a solar disk bearing the uraeus, the royal serpent symbol.

This neter can be seen as representing the victory of persistence and determination over inertia; in essence he conquers death continually. He is immortal, emerging each dawn from the underworld. The cycle of the sun can be seen as representing the ups and downs of our lives. We each go through our glorious days, sometimes descending into the 'dark night of the soul' where all seems bleak and hopeless. But life is never static. We emerge from darkness into light, wiser than we were before.

You can call upon Ra for matters of growth, self confidence, change, life cycles and rites of passage. When times are dark, meditate upon him and his celestial journey into light. You can ask for his strength upon your personal journey.

Ra Temple

In order to meet and speak with Ra, create an inner temple for him and invite him to inhabit it. It could incorporate a large sacred lake, like that at the Karnak temple complex in Egypt. It could also have an area open to the sun, where you can experience Ra's solar power, and an inner shrine representative of his voyage through the night.

You can choose to commune with Ra at any of these locations within the temple. Ra himself can be seen as having a hawk's or ram's head, or else as having a full human form.

The colours yellow and gold should predominate, and the symbols for Ra and Aaten should decorate the walls, pylons and columns of the temple. As at Karnak, you could incorporate an avenue of ram-headed sphinxes, called criosphinxes, which lead to the inner parts of the temple.

Khesu of Empowerment in the Temple of the Sun

The Temple of the Sun at Abu Simbel was built by the pharaoh Ramesses II, between 1301-1235 BC. It was dedicated to the neteru Ptah, Re Harakhte, Amon-Ra and to Ramesses himself.

Re-Harakhte (*ray*-ha-*rak*-tee) was a form of Ra combined with that of the falcon-headed neter, Horus. Re-Harakhte is the neter of the newly risen sun on the eastern horizon, and in one sense embodies youthfulness. The name means 'Horus of the Horizon'.

To access Ra's power in this form, you will visit in visualisation the temple at Abu Simbel.

Compose yourself for meditation and take yourself into the inner realms, where the landscape of Ancient Khem appears before you. You are standing in the twilight before dawn in front of the Temple of the Sun. At the front of the temple are four colossal statues of Ramsses wearing the double crown of Upper and Lower Egypt. The statues are carved directly from the rock. By the legs of the statues are other, smaller, figures, no higher than the pharaoh's knees. These represent members of his family, both male and female.

Above the entrance, is a statue of Re-Harakhte, who is falcon-headed. He holds in one hand a feather.

You pass through the entrance into a huge hypostyle hall, and here there are four statues to either side depicting Ramesses as the neter Osiris. The statues on the left wear the white crown of Upper Egypt, while those on the right wear the double crown of Upper and Lower Egypt. Bas-reliefs upon the walls show scenes of the pharoah defeating his enemies in battle.

Passing from the hypostyle hall, you enter another pillared hall, but here there are only four pillars. As you progress through the temple, so the rooms will decrease in size. The walls of the hall are decorated with scenes of offerings being made to the neteru. There is also a scene of Ramesses and and his wife Nefertari next to the sacred boats of the neteru Amun and Re-Harakhte.

You cross this hall to enter a vestibule which is the entrance to the inner sanctuary of the temple. In this place, against the back wall, are four seated statues, representing Re Harakhte, Ptah, Amon Ra and Ramesses, who saw himself as a god. Twice a year, in October and February, the rays of the sun fall into the temple directly upon these four statues, illuminating them in the solar light. The only neter who is not lit up in this way is Ptah; because of his connection with the Underwold, he remains in darkness.

Stand before the statue of Re Harakhte, and raise your arms in the Temati aui. Visualise the energy of Sekhem Heka rising through your body from the Sen-t shefat to Hati shefat. See the symbols of each degree shining within the relevant shefat. When you have enlivened Hati, draw the symbol for Ra before you in the air and say aloud:

Re-Harakhte, Re-Harakhte, Re-Harakhte

Now bend the arms at the elbow, so that they are like the arms of the symbol of Heka, and chant:

Heka, Heka, Heka

At this moment, the sun rays penetrate the temple, passing right through you, the light of Ra. As they hit the statue, it begins to glow. Through the animating principle of Heka, the presence of Ra enters the statue. He turns into a living god and from the solar disk upon his head rays of light pour down into you, entering your body at the Hati shefat. Feel the power of this energy, filling you up, making you stronger, restoring your belief in yourself.

Say:

> Re-Harakhte, Lord of the Horizon and the newly risen
> sun,
> Let your power enter into me
> That I grow strong in will and intention.
> In your image, I am capable of all things.
> I shape my world.
> I create positive change in all areas of my life.
> I attract prosperity and success in all ventures I
> undertake.
> I will this to be so.

For these moments, in your visualised temple, experience as fully as you can the sure knowledge that you are capable of these things. Imagine that all you will has already been accomplished, simply when you spoke the words aloud.

Now extend your arms once more and say:

> Re-Harakhte, I accept the gift of your power with
> thanks.

Bow to him and lower your arms. The light goes out of him and he becomes once more a statue of stone.

Leave the temple and then return to normal consciousness.

Hati Work

Hati is the seat of the will, decision-making, the projection of your power in your reality. It is assertiveness, determination and persistence. It is the ability to finish what you started, to have the courage of your convictions and to take responsibility for your actions.

We noticed something interesting when working on this part of the system. While meditating on the previous shefat and its associated neter, Isis, Simon and I had picked up on vivid imagery as well as ideas to put into the system and so on. After our first meditation on Hati, we both came out of it to say we hadn't picked much material up, and it had all seemed a bit flat. Then it dawned on us both at the same time: right, this is a shefat that needs work for both of us!

If, when working on the shefats, you have a similar experience, it will most likely be an indication that the shefat needs particular attention. In Simon's and my case, it was to do with us – at that time - having problems with our belief in our ability to change our reality. For others, the reasons might be different. But a blockage of any kind indicates a problem.

You began your shefat work with Sen-t and the basics of survival, reaching up for Khep-ti and desire. Hati is the means by which you realise these desires.

Begin your meditations by visualising the Sent-t sphere and the symbol of Heka within it, its arms reaching up towards Khep-ti. Activate Sent-t by filling it with the energy of Sekhem Heka. See its colour grow brighter; it begins to spin in a clockwise direction, shooting off rays of brilliant red light.

Now visualise Khep-ti, and place within it the symbol of Tchem Aset. Draw Sekhem Heka energy up from Sent-t to vitalise Khep-ti. See the colour grow brighter and the shefat begin to spin in a clockwise direction.

Draw the power up into Hati, and place within it the symbol of Aaten. See the shefat begin to spin and grow stronger. The energy invigorates and opens the shefat.

Meditate for some minutes upon the qualities of Hati and how they function within you and whether they need some attention. You can visit the Temple of Ra and speak with him on these matters, ask for his guidance.

Metu Terf
Principles for Inspiration and Evolution

Metu Terf (*meh*-too *turf*) means 'words of wisdom'. In third degree, you begin to work with the Sekhem Heka principles. In Reiki, there are five principles, and these augment or amplify them. The Metu Terf meditations are extensions of the khesu in the Temple of the Sun. During that khesu, you asked for Ra's power. By meditating upon the principles in Ra's temple, you work upon specific aspects of conditioning that might hold you back in life.

The Reiki Principles

Mikao Usui devised five principles by which he advocated his students should live. They are simple and sensible suggestions, and the thing I found most beautiful about them was that the words 'just for today' were included. To me, this represented we should not judge ourselves for when we slip and make mistakes. Just for today, we will try in all simplicity to live by these ideals. All we can do is live in the moment, as best we can, and not judge the past or fear for the future.

There are now many different versions of the Reiki principles, and some of them are coloured by the belief systems of the Teachers who rewrote them, but in essence, they boil down to these statements:

Just for today, I will not anger
Just for today, I will not worry
Just for today, I give thanks for all that I have
Just for today, I will work diligently with appreciation
Just for today, I will be kind to all living things

Simply saying these words aloud, at the beginning of each

day, has a positive effect upon the psyche. Because you are not trying to say 'I am going to be a better person now and forever, with no mistakes!' it is easier to accomplish the goal. And each day you renew that goal. Some days you'll be able to look back and see it was accomplished, even if on other days you couldn't help but get angry or worried, or snap at someone unkindly. The idea is that the more you repeat these affirmations, the more they become part of your living reality. I see the principle 'work diligently' as meaning working upon ourselves, whether that is through magic, Reiki or simply psychology – understanding ourselves.

The Reiki Principles promote compassion, peace, serenity and kindness. If you have already trained in Reiki or Seichim/Sekhem you should be familiar with them, and if you haven't it is worth incorporating them into your daily practice.

The Sekhem Heka Principles

We tend to be our own worst critics, sabotaging our plans and aspirations with negative thinking and conditioning, lack of self belief, lowered expectations, and by being fearful. So many people have said to me, 'I can work magic for others, but not for myself. It never works for me', or 'I want to work for myself, but feel I am being greedy or selfish'. These attitudes are guaranteed to upset any work you attempt to do for yourself.

The Sekhem Heka principles are designed to help overcome this way of thinking, which for most of us is ingrained and difficult to shift. I think it's important to first examine why these attitudes prevail.

When working magic, we have to suspend our disbelief, to immerse ourselves totally in the concept that we can change our world. This is often very hard to do, when we live in mundane reality where the magical and wondrous is not usually that apparent. As children, our minds are free and we can believe in magic very easily, but as we grow older, and conventional thinking and living is imposed upon us, so the magical can fade in our lives. To regain this wonder, we might wholeheartedly embrace belief systems that assure us we can pray, work magic, meditate, or whatever, to effect positive changes in our lives, but when it comes down to doing the work, and believing it, it's often a different matter.

The fundamental foundation of magic, and how it works, is a belief in your own will and intention. If the entire universe is comprised of energy, vibrating at different rates, then we, as beings of energy ourselves, have the ability to make changes in it. Our desires, reinforced by our will and focused intention, are forms of energy that can touch and move other forms of energy. Even from a scientific point of view, this is a simple idea. But even so, when we are assailed by the demands of mundane life, which does not operate in the quantum realms and is based very much upon empirical reality, doubt can creep in to destroy our resolve. We can be assailed by thoughts such as 'this won't make any difference, what's the point?' 'I don't have the power to do this', or 'I want to believe, but secretly I just don't think it's possible', or even 'I don't deserve this'. Faced with what seem like insurmountable problems, guilt, grief and afflictions, it's very easy to lose faith in the universe, God, Goddess, or whatever you want to call it. It's very easy to lose faith in yourself, which amounts to the same thing.

The other common form of self-sabotage is that of feeling greedy or selfish. I've heard many times the idea that when there are so many people in the world worse off than ourselves, surely it's the ultimate form of selfishness to work magically to attain more in life or to ask for help with our problems; it all seems so petty in comparison. But it's important to accept that everything is relative. We cannot grow as individuals if we are in pain, and pain can take many forms. For example, people are often reluctant to work to improve their finances, even though the fears associated with debt and keeping a roof over their heads are crippling. You are a more useful person in the world if you are free of such problems. You can help others far more effectively once you are in a secure place yourself, and the knowledge you gain upon the journey to this better place can be passed on to others.

It is also important to accept that whatever we do in life is a lesson. Sometimes we will make mistakes and bad choices. Sometimes our actions may in fact hurt others, even if we didn't intend them to. But the idea of self-evolution is being able to learn and grow from these mistakes. There is no point beating ourselves up about them; it changes nothing. No one is perfect; all we can do is attempt to live to the best of our ability and work to become more tolerant, understanding and forgiving, as well as wiser and more objective. This does not mean we have to be mushy pushovers, allowing ourselves to be doormats or whipping-posts for others, thereby feeling saintly and righteous. That's just being a martyr, and is in fact a passive-aggressive form of manipulating others. What it should mean is that we learn to view ourselves and our actions objectively in order to choose the best reactions in any situation to help ensure results we would want.

The Sekhem Heka principles promote positive thinking and self evolution:

I live in the moment
I release the fear within
I observe myself objectively
I let go of judgement
I believe in myself

Meditations Upon the Principles

For the meditations, you will visit the Temple of Ra. You should make at least five visits, and work with one principle each time. You might find you want to spend more time on one of the principles, and in that case, do so. The work shouldn't be rushed.

For Teachers: You can give an attunement after your student has completed these four meditations. The procedure is given at the end of this section.

Create ritual space using the Ankh and the Utchat, and compose yourself within it. Sit with your hands in the Tui posture.

In your mind, ask for Sekhem Heka to flow and visualise the symbols of Tcheru and the Aaten.

Visualise the ray streaming down from the universe into your body. When fully connected, stretch out your arms into the Temati position.

Imagine the Sekhem Heka ray streaming from your palms. Before you is a gateway to the universe, created by the flow of the Sekhem Heka energy.

Now, visualise your consciousness going into that gateway. Then see yourself passing beyond the gateway into a passageway of light. Walk down this passage, until you emerge into a great Hall, lined by immense columns.

The walls are decorated with wing motifs and an image of Ra stands on a dais at the far end. Go before the god and draw in the air before him the Tcheru and the Aaten symbol.

Imbue the statue with the presence and power of Ra by speaking your intention aloud. See the statue turn into a living man of great beauty. Ask him to bestow upon you the awareness to know yourself. Ask for the veils of illusion to be stripped away, and the veils of self delusion. Ask for self-awareness, for clarity, for determination, for the ability to be reborn as the sun, in knowledge. Acknowledge that from this point, there is no going back. Once you are awake to yourself, you can never sleep again. But the process is sometimes hard. It is easier to remain asleep. Acknowledge the responsibility of what you are taking on, the wisdom and determination that have brought you to this point.

For a few moments, visualise yourself, and all the different facets that make up your personality, some positive, some negative. Do not shrink from the negative traits. Try to be detached, to have no feelings about them. You are merely looking at them. Similarly, be detached about your positive traits too.

Now, think of the Sekhem Heka principle you've chosen to work upon, and how it relates to self-knowledge.

Live in the Moment

If you live in the moment, you do not fear for the future, nor judge yourself from the past. You are free to simply 'be'.

When we have undergone negative experiences or relationships, or have failed in some endeavour or another, it's natural to have these less than favourable outcomes in mind when faced with a similar problem or situation. But the fact is no two situations are really the same, and our mind set at the time has a lot to do with how we deal with them. And our mind set has a huge effect upon the outcome. While we learn from our past experiences, we can also be hampered by them. If we expect history to repeat itself, then it tends to do so, simply because we make it happen. In some perverse way, it's sometimes as if we want to prove to ourselves that things never go right, and people will always behave in a way we don't like.

If we can practice living in the moment, we can deal with situations as they arise, calling upon wisdom gained from past experience, but not making them worse with heaps of negative expectations. It's also important to remember that no two people are ever exactly the same, and what you experience with one individual might not necessarily be repeated with another. Loading a relationship (whether platonic, work-related, social, familial or romantic) with lowered expectations that derive from previous experiences does not contribute towards a desired outcome.

In meditation, you can experience in the moment how the utter freedom of living this way feels. There is no future and no past, and all the worries and anxieties connected with both do not exist.

While it may be impossible (and impractical) to maintain this feeling throughout normal everyday life, you can find this moment in meditation. You can practice viewing reality this way, so that eventually it begins to permeate your whole being. It does not solve the problems of life, of course, but helps you not to be incapacitated by them. This in turn gives a more powerful frame of mind with which to address the problems and solve them yourself.

Release the Fear Within

By fear, I do not mean the feeling inspired by being in a life or death situation faced with physical threat. I'm speaking of the inner dreads that tend to plague our lives with their constant nagging reminders that things can always go horribly wrong. Some people will even say they fear being happy, because it never lasts. Therefore, by thinking this, they make sure they're always unhappy.

Releasing fear is a product of living in the moment. So many of us live in terror – and this is mainly the fear of loss. We are concerned about our physical safety in what seems to be an increasingly violent world, our material possessions, our youth (for in Western culture youth is respected and admired more than maturity), our relationships, our work, our very existence. There is just so much we have to lose that it's hardly surprising many of us live in a constant state of anxiety about it.

We so often fear not being in control of our lives, and perhaps feel threatened by those we perceive to be more powerful in some way. We often care too deeply what others think about us, and are terrified of feeling ashamed or humiliated or beaten. Sometimes, we become so embroiled in a negative mind set we see threat and malevolence all around us. If we cannot trust anyone, we exist in a fearful state, waiting for the next deception or act of cruelty. But the fact is, we cannot rely on others for our happiness. Just about everyone is assailed by similar doubts to the ones you have, to a greater or lesser degree. It's important to bear this in mind, in any situation.

Perhaps the only people we can truly trust are ourselves – but what is trust really? It's actually attaching strings to our relationships with others. Sometimes people will act unkindly and cruelly, and we are utterly free to react to their behaviour in a positive or negative way, but sometimes, because we attach so much importance to how others view us, our expectations of people are unfairly high. We all have moments of weakness and we all make mistakes. If someone makes a mistake, it does not necessarily mean we can't trust them on any level. We do not have to fear human weakness; we can choose to view it sympathetically. Or we can simply walk away from the situation, because there is nothing to be gained from it for any party involved. Again, that is our choice.

Meditate for a few minutes on all your worries, anxieties, jealousies and insecurities. Try to see through them to their core and think about how fear could be the driving force behind them.

Look at your feelings honestly and note where the fearful lurks. Imagine any feelings of terror as actual objects – dark feathers, or black balls – and see them floating away from you, at your command. See yourself as strong and inviolate. You do not have to fear something that has not happened yet. There is no point worrying about 'what if...?' Think clearly: in this precise moment what is there to be afraid of? Believe that you can find the power within yourself to banish debilitating terrors.

Observe Yourself

To understand the motivations at the core of your being, you should begin to observe yourself carefully. It is like being a watcher in your own mind, looking at all that you say and do throughout the day. You are not there to make judgements, but simply to observe, to notice. You are looking for the mechanisms by which you deal with life's events and problems. Observe your reactions, but do not attempt to change them. Simply see them and notice them.

Imagine yourself now in a few negative situations where you react strongly. Calmly and without self-criticism, observe what you do. Think about how you react from fear, a form of self-preservation. It feels like anger, or paranoia, hurt or jealousy, but trace that feeling back to its source. See the nest of dread or panic from where it arises.

Try to trace your habitual reactions and behaviour back

in time, to when you learned to behave that way.

Let Go of Judgement

We judge others and ourselves constantly. Once we are beginning to be awake and aware, there is a tendency to be even more self-critical than before. We often disappoint ourselves, because now we can see the mechanisms at work, we think we should be totally free of them. But we have to remember that these mechanisms stem from years and years of conditioning, and will not disappear overnight. Work upon releasing the tendency to judge yourself. Simply accept what is. When you behave or react in a way that later disappoints you, observe it, note it, and then move on. Let go of the judgement, the self-punishment. You might not be able to change the past, but you will have learned from the experience. This will help you not to repeat negative behaviour patterns.

Believe in Yourself

Perhaps this is the hardest principle of all to live by. Humans tend naturally be full of self-doubt and occasionally self-loathing; exceptions do exist but are in the minority. Even someone who appears to be completely confident and strong would undoubtedly confess to occasional feelings of weakness or uncertainty should you have an intimate discussion with them about it. Working on Hati and performing the khesu in the Temple of the Sun help repair this aspect of our being.

Why is it we find it so hard to believe in ourselves? As we grow older, it is the knocks of life that tend to wither our self belief. We lose heart and hope, thereby entrenching the belief we are just victims of fate or life, and can do nothing about it. However, one thing we do have complete control over is how we react to situations and events. It is our choice to be vengeful, forgiving, tolerant, contemptuous or compassionate.

Imagine a situation where you would react strongly, and then imagine yourself reacting differently to it. Do this with several different reactions. Meditate upon the idea that a different reaction to something might ensure a result you want.

Practice, in meditation, projecting your will power and intention to achieve a specific result. Imagine that the result has already happened, simply because you have the power to affect it.

Khemt-tu Initiation and Attunement

The student should sit comfortably with their hands in the Tui posture. You summon the shining light of Sekhem Heka, by drawing Tcheru, Tcher-Sekhem and Aaten symbols in the air and visualising the ray streaming down from the cosmos. Raise your hands above your head and then sweep them down. This gesture is to bring the light down to earth.

The following is the opening statement of intent. You can use my version or adapt it to your preference:

> I call upon the mysterious ray of Sekhem Heka, in all of its power and brilliance. I call upon the adepts of the Ancient Egyptian mystery schools, to be present here and bestow their blessings upon these proceedings. I call upon the gods and goddesses of Ancient Khem, and to any guides or guardians who have a connection with those here present, to join us now, and bestow their blessings, upon Khemt-tu, this third degree Sekhem Heka initiation.

Say to the student:

> Visualise that you find yourself in the Temple of Ra, beside a great sacred lake. It is very hot and sunlight is streaming down upon you. At the end of the lake, upon a raised dais is a gigantic statue of Ra. He is shown seated upon a throne and upon his head he wears a solar disk, bearing the sign of the uraeus.
> We will now awaken the god.

Recite:

> Oh Ra, who rises in the horizon,

You rest upon law unchangeable and unalterable.
You show yourself at dawn day by day.
Your sacred boat goes forth with light;
Your radiance is upon all faces; its beams cannot be counted.
May we advance, as you advance.
May we never cease to go forward as you never cease to go forward,
Not even for a moment;
In brief seconds you pass over the spaces which we would need millions of years to travel.
You put an end to the hours of the night, and world becomes light.
Guide us through our own darknesses, oh Ra.
May we feel joy in our moments of light.
May we be aware of our continual journey and not become lost in the shadows.
We are beings of light in your image, oh Ra,
In perpetual cycles of light and darkness.

Say to the student:

You see a brilliant light emerge from the solar disk upon Ra's head, which indicates he has heard us. His statue comes alive. See him rise from his throne, a living man before you.

Now perform the attunement.

As before, simply adapt your usual attunement procedure, but incorporate the symbols Tcher-Sekhem, Tcheru and Aaten. If you wish, you could include the Ra glyph, or else perform a separate attunement to Ra energy. A full version of a suggested attunement set is given in the appendices.

When attuning the crown, visualise that you push these

symbols down into the brain stem along with the Usui ones.

When drawing the Cho Ku Rei on the palms of the hands, and 'slapping' them in, include Tcheru and Aaten also.

After the attunement, resume the visualisation.

> **Visualise Ra coming towards you. Be aware of his power, and how you too can have this power; the ability to move through changes, to constantly bring light back to your own life through your own endeavours and will. Ra holds out his hands to you, and above them dances a star.**
>
> **See the Aaten symbol come out of the star and enter your body at the Hati shefat.**
>
> **Thank Ra for the symbol, and spend a few moments communing with him. He may have important things to tell you or want to give you a symbolic gift.**

After a few minutes, call the student back from their meditation and end the session. Affirm that the initiation is complete.

Khem-tu Healing Session

Use the Aaten symbol upon yourself and others in a healing session.

As with the previous shefats, begin the healing by opening Sen-t and Khep-ti. Then progress to Hati.

Focus upon issues connected with self assertion, will power, application to a project, self evolution and the ability to walk with strength and certainty through the peaks and troughs of life. Intend for the symbol to enhance your will power and your ability to affect changes in your reality.

Ftu-Nu
The Fourth Degree

The fourth degree concerns Ab, the heart shefat. The neter associated with Ftu-Nu is Bast, in her aspect of goddess of love. The symbol for Bast is a hieroglyph of a perfume jar. The name of the perfume jar is Nekhnem, which also means the actual perfume or unguent. As perfume is such an important part of interacting with Bast, the use of incense and sweet aromas form part of this degree.

Part of this degree concerns acceptance and forgiveness associated with being hurt and suffering emotional pain. The main focus of Ab is the evolution of unconditional love, but from my own experience with students and clients, I know that a great many people suffer from unresolved hurts, conflicts and losses; it is the main reason that people come for healing sessions. These are issues that really need to be sorted out before moving on to giving unconditionally to all. Therefore, I have included in this tier various khesus and meditations to address problems associated with grief, loss and forgiveness.

The majority of us have unresolved issues concerning these aspects of life, quite often stemming back to the distant past. And many people also find it difficult to let go of this pain; it haunts them, perhaps buried and suppressed, but, like a ghost, with a tendency to walk at midnight when all is quiet.

This system is written for the benefit of newcomers to this kind of work as well as seasoned veterans of energy healing and magic. It might be that you have already addressed and worked upon some of the issues that are focused upon in Ftu-Nu. If you are fortunate enough to be in the position where there are no negative emotional concerns in your life that require in depth healing, the exercises of Ftu-Nu concerned with issues of forgiveness and acceptance can be performed to help others. Even if your life is in harmony, you doubtlessly know others who have not yet reached that state.

But Ftu-Nu is not just about the healing of pain; it also the experience and expression of pure joy and love – the raw and radiant energy of them.

Deficiency in the Ab shefat leads to a cold, withdrawn and anti-social personality, someone who might have an obsessive fear of relationships. Quite often this is because of past emotional traumas, so that the individual has lost faith in love itself. Prone to loneliness and depression, they cut themselves off from the rest of the world, and tend to be intolerant and judgmental of other people.

An over-active Ab is quite the opposite, giving rise to the demanding, jealous type, who is insecure emotionally, requiring more and more love from their partners, and the proof to go with it, which of course can rarely be satisfied. Such types tend to be overly reliant on others for their own happiness and often become trapped in co-dependent relationships with similar types.

A balanced Ab nourishes a compassionate and empathetic individual, who understands the importance of loving the self in order to extend that emotion to others. They would not be clingy, looking to their partners to sustain their emotional health. Relationships to them are a graceful act of two-way giving that nourishes both. Secure in their feelings, those with a healthy Ab radiate compassion to all around them.

The Aui of Ftu-Nu - Pesh-Ti
(*pesh*-tee)

The aui of this degree is pesh-ti, which means 'the two halves of heaven'. In this position, the fingertips of the hands rest lightly against each other, barely touching, while the palms are slightly cupped. It stimulates the energy flow, which empowers you during meditation and ritual.

Pesh-ti is a gentle aui. When you sit with your hands in this position, focus upon letting go of 'heavy' feelings. Let the light of Sekhem Heka bloom between your loosely cupped palms; it is light in both senses. Nurture this lightness and direct it into the Ab shefat, so that your heart centre also grows light. Use this energy to help dispel lethargy, heaviness, melancholy and heartache.

Meditation Upon the Per-Ahu Symbol

This symbol derives from the ancient hieroglyph for a human heart, and its name means 'house of the heart'. The House of the Heart was also another name for the Judgment Hall of Osiris.

Per-Ahu Meditation for the Attuned

Compose yourself for meditation and connect with Sekhem Heka energy through the Tcheru.

Clear your mind and then visualise the Per-Ahu symbol shining before you. Spend some time gazing inwardly upon it, and see what ideas come to you concerning its use for you personally, or any personal meanings for it.

Place your hands over your heart shefat for a self healing and keep visualising Per-Ahu. Use it to promote compassion, emotional understanding, emotional maturity and the ability to forgive. The light of this shefat is green. Imagine this radiance fills your being.

Experiment with using the Per-Ahu symbol in conjunction with the Usui sending symbol, or if you have not reached second degree, simply by connecting with the energy and using the symbol as you 'beam' it.

Per-Ahu Meditation for the Non-Attuned

Compose yourself for meditation and connect with Sekhem Heka energy through the Tcheru.

Clear your mind and then visualise the Per-Ahu symbol shining before you. Spend some time gazing inwardly upon it, and see what ideas come to you concerning its use for you personally, or any personal meanings for it. Visualise the green radiance of the Ab shefat filling your being.

Draw the symbol in the air before you and say its name three times. As you do so, intend this symbol to represent your ability to feel, to forgive, to be compassionate. It symbolises the wisdom of emotional security and unconditional love. But these aspects do not mean sentimentality. Wise love has its eyes open to reality.

Meditate for some minutes upon Per-Ahu. Concentrate upon feeling unconditional love and what this truly means. Connect with the compassion represented by the symbol; compassion for all living things, including yourself.

Communing with Bast

Originally, the cat-headed Bast was a solar lioness-headed neter. But over the centuries, she transformed into the more familiar version. The Greeks were largely responsible for her acquiring a lunar aspect, since they equated her with their goddess Artemis. Bast was a neter of the common people more than kings and queens. She was associated with protection of the home and of children. She enjoyed perfume, dancing and music. Her festivals, as reported by historians of the time, were reputedly quite orgiastic in nature.

Although Bast does have a feline nature, and can claw as well as purr, she is seen as less ferocious and fiery than lioness goddesses such as Sekhmet. However, as any cat, she can be quite vicious, especially in cases of protection.

The reason she is placed at the heart in this system is quite deliberate. Some might say the goddess Hathor, typically identified with love, would be more appropriate. But to me, Bast had to be the one, and this is partly to do with my personal view on how Bast has developed as a goddess in modern times.

There is a tendency within some systems to deny or filter the darker aspects of life, people and the world. The desired view of life, and how best to think and behave, sometimes advocates what I see as a cloying 'niceness', including the aspects of powerful goddesses like Bast. Love has claws as well as fluffy fur. And it is not just about sentimentality. Sometimes the heart has to be tough, even if it isn't hard. Bast is a goddess of love, joy and sensual pleasure, but she also has great strength and will defend ferociously those in her care. In life, sometimes we have to do this too, and our hearts have to be strong. I think it's important to differentiate between honest love and compassion and sugary and shallow sentimentality.

The Moon Temple of Bast

As for the other neteru of the previous degrees, you should create a temple for Bast and ask her to reside within it. It should be visited in moonlight and its stones should sparkle in this light. Beyond the first pylon, there is a sacred pool, surrounded by fragrant trees. The inner rooms of the temple beyond are lit only by moonlight and dim lamps. The air is heavily perfumed. The colour green should be predominant and the symbols for Bast and Per-Ahu. The statue of Bast within the temple should be made of silver and show her in a seated position. When you have created your temple and have asked Bast to take up residence within it, perform the following meditation.

Compose yourself for meditation and visualise that you go back to Ancient Khem. It is night time and the moon is full. Ahead of you is the temple of Bast, its tall columns pale in the moonlight. You pass beneath the blue shadow of the entrance pylon and find  yourself in the courtyard. Pause to drink from the pool, where the moon is reflected. The scent of the trees is very strong. You can see the symbol for Bast's name carved into the walls and columns of the buildings.

All around you roam the sacred cats of Bast, who live within the temple. Some are sleeping, others prowling in and out of the shadows, yet more playing with fallen blossoms from the trees. From within the temple you hear the faint sound of music being played, a woman's voice singing.

The feelings conjured by this environment are those of serenity and acceptance. In this place, there is no strife, no anxiety. Your heart fills with a love that is indescribable. It is the love of infinity, the ultimate, the universe itself. In the embrace of this feeling is unending hope, sureness that ultimately all things are resolved and completed. Even when you experience unhappiness and difficulty, these things are merely steps upon the path to understanding and wisdom. Be thankful for these lessons. In Bast's temple, you can cast off the dark garments of harsh things in life that might assail you. Here, you are free to be at peace.

Walk now to the inner sanctum of the temple. The air is sweet with incense smoke. In the shrine is the seated statue of Bast made entirely of silver. The rays of the moon fall upon it, making it gleam.

Stand before Bast and place your arms in the Temati posture. Say:

Oh, Bast, Lady of Asheru, Ruler of Sekhet-neter,
Ruler of the Divine Field, Lady of Ankhtawy,
Life of the Two Lands.
Hear me, awaken to my presence.
May the heka of your divine spirit enter into this statue before me.
Awaken my heart
Teach my soul
Protect my body
Grant me the wisdom of the heart.

The statue of Bast becomes enlivened with her presence, and begins to glow more brightly. She stands up and approaches you. In her eyes, you see all the things that you aspire to, and you realise that she is in fact a mirror. She is part of you.

Take Bast's hands in yours and chant:

Pekhat ha-t merut (pek-*at* hah-*tay* meh-*root*)

This means 'wise love'. As you chant it softly, visualise that all negative feelings you might hold are transformed into higher frequencies of energy. What is petty becomes radiant. You are filled with the light of Bast and can rise above trivial matters. You are given the perspective to view things from a distance, with objectivity.

Place your hands in the pesh-ti position and let a ball of energy form between your palms. Infuse it, by intention, with the light of Bast and then place this light into your Ab shefat.

Spend some time communing with Bast, and when you are ready, return to normal consciousness.

Ab Work

When working on Ab, begin by enlivening the other shefats, starting with Sen-t. The energy vitalises the red shefat of survival, rising through the orange of desire and creativity, through the golden yellow of projected will into the green heart centre. Ab can be seen as the first of the 'higher' shefats. After concerns of the inner self, the energy now reaches outwards to embrace the universe. Projected will without compassion and empathy can be tyrannical; Hati needs the subtle emanations of Ab to remain stable and just.

Quite often, we have experiences with others that scar us deeply, and it is very hard to forgive and let go of the negative feelings surrounding the situation. Similarly, we might harbour feelings of regret and guilt over past actions and find it hard to forgive ourselves. Working on Ab helps with these issues. Part of this degree involves a khesu to address and resolve them.

When working with Ab, you can concentrate on your connectedness with all other living beings, through the medium of universal energy. Visualise the 'flame' of your heart shefat and work upon strengthening it, imagining that it grows brighter within you. It is important to love yourself as much as extending compassion to others. Spend some time nurturing yourself, pampering in a meditational sense, by feeding the Ab shefat with energy.

Ftu-Nu Initiation and Attunement

The student should sit comfortably with their hands in the Tui posture. You summon the shining light of Sekhem Heka, by drawing the Tcheru, Tcher-Sekhem and Per-Ahu symbols in the air and visualising the ray streaming down from the cosmos. Raise your hands above your head and then sweep them down. This gesture is to bring the light down to earth.

The following is the opening statement of intent. You can use my version or adapt it to your preference:

> I call upon the mysterious ray of Sekhem Heka, in all of its power and brilliance. I call upon the adepts of the Ancient Egyptian mystery schools, to be present here and bestow their blessings upon these proceedings. I call upon the gods and goddesses of Ancient Khem, and to any guides or guardians who have a connection with those here present, to join us now, and bestow their blessings, upon Ftu-nu, this fourth degree Sekhem Heka initiation.

Say to the student:

> Visualise that you find yourself in the Temple of Bast. You stand before a statue of Bast. In one hand she holds an ankh, symbol of life, and in another the sistrum, the rattle that is sacred to her. We will call to her and awaken her.

Recite:

> Oh, Bast, Lady of Asheru, Ruler of Sekhet-neter,
> Lady of Ankhtawy, Ruler of the Divine Field,
> Life of the Two Lands.

We call to you.
Hear us and awaken to our presence.
Bast, you are beauty, health and gentleness.
You comfort those who are made mad by the moon,
When you walk at their side in the shadow lands.
You, oh lady, are of the gods who protect this world.
Thunder and lightning strike the skies,
But you return in glory with your father, the sun.
You can blast and you can forgive
You can punish and you can reward
You can grant sunshine unto children
You can grant moonshine unto lovers
You have died and yet you live.
It is whispered that if one man or woman should believe in your power
You can hearken to the prayers of all the world.
Hear us, oh Bast,
You can twist the skein and weave the thread of destiny.
You are sacred and beautiful, a lady of music.
You are lustrous and all-powerful,
And the world rides upon the arch of your back.
You are venerated and called the Lady of the East.
Bast the divine, ruler of the night, goddess of love,
Infinite, all-wise and all-knowing.
Grant blessings unto us who follows in your ways.
Great cat, who is the cat of the heavens,
Grant to us our desires. Be favourable unto us.

Say to the student:

You see a brilliant light emerge from the ankh in Bast's hand, which indicates she has heard us. Her statue comes alive. She gazes into your eyes and her expression is full of compassion.

Now perform the attunement.

As before, simply adapt your usual attunement procedure, but incorporate the symbols Tcher-Sekhem, Tcheru and Per-Ahu. If you wish, you could include the Bast glyph, or else perform a separate attunement to Bast's energy. A full version of a suggested attunement set is given in the appendices.

When attuning the crown, visualise that you push these symbols down into the brain stem along with the Usui ones.

When drawing the Cho Ku Rei on the palms of the hands, and 'slapping' them in, include Tcheru and Per-Ahu also.

After the attunement, resume the visualisation.

> **Visualise Bast coming towards you. Be aware of her power, and how it is mirrored within you. Your heart is strong, your feelings true. Bast holds out her hands to you, and above them dances a star.**
> **See the Per-Ahu symbol come out of the star and enter your body at the Ab shefat.**
> **Thank Bast for the symbol, and spend a few moments communing with her. She may have important things to tell you or want to give you a symbolic gift.**

After a few minutes, call the student back from their meditation and end the session. Affirm that the initiation is complete.

The Vales of Pain
Dark Matters of the Heart

The ability to forgive those who harm us is seen as a desirable attribute in the majority of spiritual systems. The fact that it's needed perhaps illustrates how much like growing children the bulk of humanity is. We might think we're mature, wise and capable, but quite often our interactions aren't that different from the altercations of the playground. We hurt and get hurt; it's a part of life. We are naturally competitive beings, and have a tendency to be territorial; these aspects often give rise to conflict. Like any beast of the wild, we will defend our patch, whether that's our position in a social scene, our status, our beliefs, our perceived expertise, our relationships or our sphere of influence. So quite often the instinct to lash out is simply an ingrained form of self preservation.

Individuals lacking in empathy, who are unable (or unwilling) to put themselves in the position of others, will unwittingly cause pain, merely because they cannot identify with the results of their actions. In such situations, when challenged, the individuals might be genuinely perplexed and confused, and quite often see themselves as the 'demonised' victims, ignorant of any stream of casualties they might have left in their wakes.

Bearing these things in mind, part of forgiveness is to appreciate that sometimes people act carelessly rather than cruelly. There will be occasions in life when you come across someone who's well aware of what they're doing and simply doesn't care, or is warped and twisted enough to take pleasure in giving pain, or believe it's the right thing to do. But objectively that is not as common as those who act unconsciously from ignorance, fear, pain, jealousy or paranoia.

We might also carry resentment with us from our childhoods; the way that family, teachers or other influential adults treated and affected us. The scars of these wounds are often thin, over unhealed flesh. It can take very little to reopen them. How do we find it within ourselves to forgive those who have actually damaged us, deliberately or otherwise? It can take us a lifetime to get over the psychological wounds adults inflicted (usually in ignorance) upon us when we were children.

In my view, taking responsibility for ourselves does a lot to help heal us. We might not have been responsible for any hurt that was inflicted on us, but we can be responsible for how we deal with its aftermath. It's very easy to be a wilting victim, bleating 'it's not my fault, it's not fair', but that achieves nothing. Surely, the best thing is to rediscover strength and esteem, not to wallow in self pity, blaming others for everything. And maybe, just maybe, during conflicts in adult life, we ourselves contribute to the situations through our negative expectations, confusing signals or inability to communicate. It could be argued that the conditioning we received as children created who we are, complete with our weaknesses, so those adults who affected us then are still to blame. But if we can just be aware of that fact, we can change how we react to situations. We don't have to be chained to the past or any ogres lurking there who affected us.

Some people find it easier to forgive than others, but ultimately hot, seething feelings of resentment and bitterness harm us more than the object of those feelings. If someone hurts you badly, you might be chewing yourself to pieces reliving events, but they might not be thinking about it at all. Who's feeling worse? Who is still suffering? In that situation, you are merely piling more pain on top of what you already feel. Maybe whoever hurt you doesn't deserve your forgiveness, but you deserve the release you can achieve once you can cut yourself free of those feelings.

People will often say to others who are still brooding over a particular hurt: 'Move on! Get over it!' I don't think this advice is at all helpful, and if anything is slightly insulting. If you feel something very deeply, you can't just shrug it off and 'move on' as if nothing happened. Sometimes, you might be struggling with as to why it happened, or have no sense of closure. Dealing with these situations is more complex than simply trying to follow the advice of 'get over it!'

Unless you can have a frank and honest discussion with the person or people who hurt or offended you, the chances are you might never fully understand why a negative situation occurred. Both parties need to have a willingness to discuss it, and your desire to understand might not be enough for someone to want to get into such a dialogue. Also, the people concerned might not still be in your life. In such cases, you need to accept the situation, and that too is often very difficult. If you are a practitioner of magic, or an energy healer, you have these resources at your disposal to help you overcome the less pleasant events and situations in life. Sometimes, these resources are hampered by the self-sabotaging tendencies mentioned in the previous degree. Grief can take a long time to get over. Sometimes there are things to forgive, in ourselves and in others. But how do you address these things when you are still full of volcanic emotion?

Sutcha
The Art of the Strengthened Heart
(*soo*-tcha)

Sutcha means, in Ancient Egyptian, to make strong, to make healthy, to refresh, to heal, to save or to protect. I think it's also interesting that in sound it resembles the English word 'suture', which is used to heal a wound.

Before you can bestow forgiveness, you have to want to and mean it. It would be very easy simply to say the words in a ritual format and beam energy into a situation, but if your heart isn't in it, if deep inside you're still angry and bleeding, it's a meaningless gesture. It's also important to bear in mind that anger is a phase of grief, and you need to let it run its course. It's not 'bad' to feel it; in some ways it can help you through a dark time. Perform sutcha, and any subsequent rite, only when you feel ready to: when it feels right.

To perform sutcha, open your ab shefat and draw the light of Sekhem Heka into it. Call upon Bast to empower this light. Do not strain to banish negative emotions or transform them into positive ones. Simply put your trust in the energy and ask for Bast to bring healing to you. Similarly, do not expect or wish for any particular outcome. This is an act of letting go. Not consciously letting go of the pain or the emotions, but merely allowing the energy to flow through you, to do its work.

Sit with your hands in the au-taa position, your body relaxed. Say to yourself:

> **I open myself to the energy of Sekhem Heka, to heal all issues of the heart. Abakh tep merrut.**
> (ab-*akh* tep meh-*root*)

These last three words mean to 'forget in love'. You can chant them softly. Again, do not invest the words with any expectation of outcome. Concentrate on living in the moment and the moment only. Do not think about anything. Focus only on the green light in your ab shefat and its warmth. Trust that the energy and the intention behind the words, programmed into them during the creation of this system, will do their work regardless of any resentments or negative feelings that might sabotage the work.

Repeat sutcha for as long as you feel is necessary. You can do this once a week, or daily if you prefer. Keep an eye on yourself, and if you feel at any time overwhelmed, refrain from sutcha until you feel balanced again. During this time, you may perform hands on healing on yourself or simply draw Sekhem Heka into your shefats.

For those who are working for others, perform the sutcha with these people in mind and ask for the energy to work for them. Visualise them clearly, their ab shefats full of the healing green radiance. At the same time, chant 'abakh tep merrut' for them.

It is usually regarded as essential to obtain people's permission before performing energy work for them. If at all possible, do this beforehand. But sometimes you'll find yourself wanting to help in a situation where it is impossible to obtain this permission. In these cases, ask Sekhem Heka that the work you are doing will be for the highest good of all, and will only affect the person/people concerned if it is their higher selves' wish to accept it. Otherwise, the energy will simply be a non-invasive positive influence around them and their situations.

Khesu Naa

(*keh*-soo nah)

This khesu is a rite of passage, similar to an initiation. This is because it represents a rebirth. Naa in Ancient Egyptian had several meanings, two of which are 'to show pity' and 'to sail away from'. As forgiveness is certainly an act of sailing away from pain, this seemed the most pertinent term. It was interesting that when I was scouring dictionaries to find words that 'spoke' to me for this book, none of the synonyms for forgiveness and mercy existed in the books. The nearest I could get to the meaning I was looking for was 'pity'. It's perhaps worth contemplating why the Ancient Egyptians had so few words for the concept of forgiving.

When you can forgive someone or something, it means you have really turned a corner, found a brighter path in life. It is the second part of healing. The first part is being able to forgive and mean it.

Therefore, there is a full khesu for this procedure, which should be undertaken with the solemnity and dedication of an initiation.

The khesu is written primarily for those wishing to get over a severed relationship of any kind, when the people concerned are no longer in their lives yet are still emotionally attached. If you are in a situation where someone you want to forgive is still a part of your life, and you wish them to remain so, the wording and imagery can be adapted, to exclude the severance aspect.

Create your sacred space as you would for an attunement.

Sit comfortably with your hands in the Tui posture.

Summon the shining light of Sekhem Heka, by drawing the Tcheru and Per-Ahu symbols in the air and visualising the ray streaming down from the cosmos. Raise your hands above your head and then sweep them down. This gesture is to bring the light down to earth.

Say:

> I call upon the mysterious ray of Sekhem Heka, in all of its power and brilliance. I call upon the gods and goddesses of Ancient Khem, and to any guides or guardians who have a connection with me to join with me now and bestow their blessings upon me, and upon this sacred rite, this khesu of forgiveness.

Now visualise yourself in the Temple of Bast, standing before her statue. Call to her and awaken her.

Recite:

> Oh, Bast, Lady of Asheru, Ruler of Sekhet-neter,
> Lady of Ankhtawy, Ruler of the Divine Field,
> Life of the Two Lands.
> I call to you.
> Hear me and awaken to my presence.
> Bast, you are beauty, health and gentleness.
> You comfort those who are made mad by the moon,
> When you walk at their side in the shadow lands.
> You, oh lady, are of the gods who protect this world.
> Thunder and lightning strike the skies,
> But you return in glory with your father, the sun.
> You can blast and you can forgive
> You can punish and you can reward
> You can grant sunshine unto children
> You can grant moonshine unto lovers
> You have died and yet you live.

It is whispered that if one man or woman should
believe in your power
You can hearken to the prayers of all the world.
Hear me, oh Bast,
You can twist the skein and weave the thread of
destiny.
You are sacred and beautiful, a lady of music.
You are lustrous and all-powerful,
And the world rides upon the arch of your back.
You are venerated and called the Lady of the East.
Bast the divine, ruler of the night, goddess of love,
Infinite, all-wise and all-knowing.
Grant blessings unto me who follows in your ways.
Great cat, who is the cat of the heavens,
Grant to me my desire. Be favourable unto me.

See the ankh in Bast's hand begin to glow with radiance,
and visualise that her statue comes to life. When she gazes
into your eyes, she sees your heart; she knows why you are
here before her.

Say:

Divine Bast, listen to my words
I am here before you to grant forgiveness to *
(person)
For * (what they did)
Let my heart be light
Let my inner being radiate the light of forgiveness
For we, the children of this world, act in ignorance
May your hands be upon my shoulders, Oh Bast,
As I walk from my own vale of shadow
May your light banish the shadows
For I am a free being
I cut the cord between me and *
I am free to walk my own path

And I forgive * in truth.
Abakh tep merrut.

Now raise your arms into the Temati position and, without straining, gently beam Sekhem Heka out towards the object of your forgiveness. As this occurs, see also any cords of connection severing between you. If you wish to, use a visualised blade to cut them, or break them with your bare hands. You are not letting the person/people go: you are freeing yourself from them.

When this is done, and all the cords are severed, bring your hands together in the Tui posture.

Say:

So, it is done.
I have done my part
And accept what is and will be.

Stand up and take a step forward. Visualise that the flaking black ashes of a shadow self are left behind you. You are shining with the light of Sekhem Heka, truly free. Shake yourself like an animal. Laugh aloud.

Visualise that a spirit wind comes and blows the ashes away. It blows through you, empowering the light of Sekhem Heka within you.

See your heart shefat shining brilliantly like a bright green star. The rays of this light spiral out from your being into the universe. For some moments visualise yourself as thousands of feet tall: a god or goddess striding among the stars. This is your path. No one can stop you. Nothing from the past can haunt or hurt you. You are bigger than anything that used to hold you back.

And you forgive.

To end the khesu, thank Bast for her presence and visualise her turning back into a statue of stone. For a few moments, give thanks to yourself that every experience in life is a lesson that makes you wiser and stronger, even though it sometimes doesn't feel like that at the time.

When you have concluded the meditation, celebrate. Eat or drink something you really love, or if you have shared the experience of the khesu with friends, indulge in a party.

Nekhnem Khesu
San Ab

Nekhnem (*nek*-nem) is a word for perfume. San Ab means to anoint the heart. Bast is strongly associated with perfume, and it played a great part in her rites in ancient times. Even the hieroglyph of her name incorporates a perfume jar.

Perfume promotes positive feelings. It is worn on the body to make the wearer more appealing – a sweet scent is believed to attract potential love partners. It is burned in the home as oil or incense to improve the atmosphere. Everyone wants a fragrant home, and we have countless brands of air fresheners to help accomplish that.

Different scents also have different associations – they can be seen as almost as powerful as words.

This is a khesu of lightened being, and can be performed a week or so after a khesu of forgiveness. For those who have not performed that particular khesu, Nekhnem Khesu can be performed any time, simply to be enjoyed.

To perform this rite, wear clothes that will allow you to draw with oil upon your breastbone area. If this is not possible, you can draw upon the wrists instead. You will need some perfume oil that you find particularly appealing. Through your enjoyment of its scent, Bast will also enjoy it.

Create your sacred space and compose yourself for meditation within it. Call upon Sekhem Heka to flow through you and for some moments stand in the Temati position, visualising the energy streaming into your body and filling it.

Call upon Bast, either using an invocation of your own invention or utilising some of the words of the rites given above.

See Bast standing before you, her eyes full of compassion and understanding.

Say:

> Oh Bast, great cat of the heavens
> I perform here the rite of San Ab – the anointing of the heart
> As you preside over matters of the heart
> Open my heart centre to the love of the universe
> Let it flow into me and heal me
> Let it warm me.

Pour some of the oil into your hands and gently rub it into the palms. Sit with your hands in the pesh-ti position, held before the Ab shefat, and feel the warmth of Sekhem Heka bringing out the scent of the oil. Imagine this as a greenish light forming between your hands.

Softly chant:

> **Netchemu netchem ab** (*netch*-em-oo, *netch*-em, *ab*)

The first word means love, joy, sweetness, sweet smelling, and netchem ab means to rejoice, to be happy

As you recite these words, focus upon bringing that feeling into your Ab shefat. Experience moments of utter sweetness, a pure joy of life and love. These moments are separate from the concerns of everyday life. They are a respite from all the trivial worries that might assail you.

Visualise that Bast partakes in and augments this process.

The green light grows brighter and fills your sacred space. It envelops both Bast and you, so that your energy becomes one with hers, and the limitless love of the neter fills your being.

Now dip a finger into the oil and draw on your chest the symbol of the perfume jar, part of Bast's name. When this is done, visualise that the green light around you is drawn into your Ab shefat. Feel its warmth centred there. Experience this for some moments, visualising that the energy is healing and strengthening your Ab shefat. It is wiping away past hurts, bringing hope for the future.

To complete this working, beam the energy out into the world through your raised hands. Experience your connectedness with all things.

When you are ready to finish, place your hands over the Ab shefat. As you do this, bid farewell to Bast and see her disappear.

Ftu-Nu Healing Session

Use the Per-Ahu symbol upon yourself and others in a healing session, beginning by working through the lower shefats as previously described.

Work upon issues connected with emotions and feelings, and the ability to experience love and to accept it. If appropriate, the Ab shefat can be worked upon concerning issues of forgiveness and releasing a recipient from emotional pain.

Intend for the symbol to enhance your capacity for compassion, tolerance, understanding and unconditional love.

Tu-Nut
The Fifth Degree

Tu-nut concerns Ashash-t (aah-*shash*-tay), the throat shefat, which is the seat of communication and expression. The neter associated with this degree is Maat, the goddess of cosmic order and truth. Her symbol was the feather, which was also a part of her head-dress.

The Ancient Egyptians strove to 'live in Maat', which meant essentially 'living in truth'. But from our own experiences in life, we eventually come to the realisation there is no 'ultimate truth', only 'subjective truths'. Our personal truths may change from day to day, as we change as individuals. We can aim only to be true to ourselves, to the best of our ability, while aware of the mutability of life, thoughts, opinions and principles.

In mythology, the heart of a deceased person was weighed upon the scales of Anubis in the Hall of the Two Truths in the Underworld. In the other pan of the scales rested the feather of Maat. If the heart was true, then the deceased progressed to the Land in the West, Amenti, the Egyptian interpretation of heaven. If the heart failed this test, the deceased would be devoured by monsters of the Underworld. We can view this symbolically as representing how if we are not true to ourselves, we risk being devoured by our own delusions and deceits. To live in 'not-truth', or to live in denial, cannot ultimately make us happy.

In this degree you work upon your personal Maat, your ability to 'live in truth'. The shefat of this degree is concerned with communication, but also with silence. Communication can be as much about what is not said as about what is said.

When Ashash-t is deficient, we find the shy, reticent individual who is afraid to speak up and perhaps believes people will just think their ideas are stupid. They most likely have a difficult expressing their thoughts and feelings into words and therefore get misunderstood. Often they probably don't even get heard since their voices will be soft and ineffective.

On the other hand, the over-active Ashash-t gives us the loud voiced person who has to dominate every conversation. They have an inability to listen to others and it might seem that in any social interaction they don't take in a word of what others say and are simply waiting for their next turn to say something, usually taking it quite forcefully by interrupting!

The balanced Ashash-t leads someone who is both a good speaker and a good listener. Their voice will be pleasant upon the ears. These are generally very creative people in some way, who can communicate beautifully, not only their thoughts but also their feelings and dreams. Having a 'good ear' is an aspect of a healthy Ashash-t, so many musicians will be found with fully-functioning throat shefats.

Dancers and actors also come into this category, since graceful and controlled physical movement is also an aspect of a healthy Ashash-t. A good actor has to express whatever character they play convincingly, through body movement and the voice.

The Aui of Tu-Nut – Uba-Ab
(*oo*-bah ab)

The aui of this degree is uba-ab, which means to open the heart, to speak freely. The little fingers are bent inwards over the palms to meet the thumbs. Other fingers remain straight.

Use this aui when meditating upon the Tchet-it symbol, the feather of Maat or when communing with Maat.

Meditation Upon the Tchet-It Symbol

Tchet-It Meditation for the Attuned

Compose yourself for meditation and connect with Sekhem Heka energy through the Tcheru.

Clear your mind and then visualise the Tchet-it symbol shining before you. Spend some time gazing inwardly upon it, and see what ideas come to you concerning its use for you personally, or any personal meanings for it.

Place your hands over your throat shefat for a self healing and keep visualising Tchet-it. Use it to help you express yourself honestly, to communicate ideas, feelings and thoughts with clarity. Imagine that the pure blue radiance of this symbol fills your being. In the light of this radiance, energy that might have become blocked and clogged up within the shefat, resulting from bitten back words and suppressed feelings, is released.

Place your hands in the uba-ab posture. Speak aloud things you have never spoken before. Cleanse yourself of repressed words.

Experiment with using the Tchet-it symbol in conjunction with the Usui sending symbol, or if you have not reached second degree, simply by connecting with the energy and using the symbol as you 'beam' it.

Tchet-it Meditation for the Non-Attuned

Compose yourself for meditation and connect with Sekhem Heka energy through the Tcheru. Place your hands in the uba-ab posture.

Clear your mind and then visualise the Tchet-it symbol shining before you. Spend some time gazing inwardly upon it, and see what ideas come to you concerning its use for you personally, or any personal meanings for it.

Draw the symbol in the air before you and say its name three times. As you do so, intend this symbol to represent your power to communicate effectively and to express yourself. Visualise that any energy that has become blocked and trapped in the throat shefat, as a result from words you might have bitten back, is now released. You are free to speak aloud things you have never spoken aloud before. Free yourself of repressed words.

Meditate for some minutes upon having the ability to express yourself with clarity and honesty.

A Word on Magical Ethics

Unless we live like hermits, there is no doubt that other people play a great part in how our lives progress. We can work upon ourselves with diligence, become stronger, less fearful and more confident and compassionate, but ultimately we will always come across situations in life where the actions of others have an effect upon us. In order to preserve ourselves or protect others, we might feel we need to take action that will detrimentally affect another. What then are the ethical implications of working magic to help in such situations?

Generally speaking, the majority of magical schools and traditions have a firm rule that no one should impose their will upon another person. Everyone should have free will. However, some schools will say that you can impose your will upon another only to the point where they will do something they would have done anyway, or would like to do, either consciously or sub-consciously.

As to how the Egyptians viewed the concept of magical ethics, they did have taboos that it was considered wrong to cross. However, they did not have a concept of 'sin', or believe that people afflicted with misfortune were being punished for past actions. They understood that 'innocent' people could as easily be struck by random forces of chaos as those who might be seen to deserve it. The Ancient Egyptians did believe that people should be responsible for their own actions and that those actions had a bearing on later life, not to mention how they were judged after death in the Hall of the Two Truths. That was part of the idea of 'living in Maat', and in some ways is similar to the Asian belief of 'karma'.

It's important to remember though that ethics differ according to culture and beliefs. What might be considered unethical for one set of people might for another set be well within the bounds of what is acceptable. What is ethical for one person might be 'sinful' for another. In this sense, ethics are entirely a subjective human construction, tied up with the dualistic idea of right and wrong. The universe is not ethical or moral, it just is. Ideas of ethics stem from humans struggling to live companionably with one another, and to encourage order in society rather than chaos.

When working magic, bear in mind the idea of living in Maat – cosmic harmony. If a situation arises where you intend to inflict your will upon another, think carefully before doing so, and be fully prepared to accept the consequences of your actions, whatever they might be, and whenever and however they might manifest. If you're not harming anyone else, do what you will, as many magical schools will tell you. But if your actions might harm someone else (even just in the sense of a situation turning out more in yours or someone else's favour than theirs), and you still feel you have good reason to proceed, take responsibility for what you do. Do not randomly smite – this is just acting out vengeance, and does not involve trying to restore harmony. Generally, if something occurs in life where you feel hotly that you need to take extreme action, it's best to let yourself cool down for a couple of days before doing anything. Quite often, you'll feel differently then, and although you might still take magical action, it will be more measured and less governed by emotion.

As you work your magic, ask that the outcome is for the highest good of all concerned. Do not intend for it to harm for the sake of harm. As a 'safety precaution', you can start your working by stating that you are acting to the best of your knowledge, and if you are wrong then ask that the truth be shown to you and that the work you do shall then have no effect. As the old saying goes, sometimes you might have to be cruel to be kind, but as another old saying goes: do as you would be done by.

Communing with Maat

Maat was depicted as a beautiful young woman who was crowned with an ostrich plume. This symbol is used to represent the *heka* of Maat in Sekhem Heka. Visualise it to access her energy. She is generally shown in the form of a woman, with outstretched wings. In one hand she holds a sceptre, in the other an ankh. Maat was closely associated with the ibis-headed neter Thoth (Tehuti in Egyptian), who was believed to be the inventor of all arts and sciences, and who presided over scribes and knowledge. Thoth was often called upon as a peace-maker when certain neteru were in conflict, because of his just wisdom. He shares many of Maat's attributes.

To commune with Maat is to connect with truth, which can often be painful. There are many things we seek to hide from ourselves; thoughts and emotions that make us uncomfortable. We can be weighed down with guilt and regrets, things we might seek to bury and forget, but which have a habit of resurfacing to plague us. To live in Maat, in truth, means to confront these things. They are our personal demons and part of having power over them is simply having the courage to face and name them. The image we can use to confront perhaps some of the ugliest things in our lives is that of a most beautiful creature. If we can be this beauty, this being of no artifice, so we can shine with the light of Maat and project this light into our lives.

Another aspect of Maat is justice and order. Therefore, in the Way of Maat, we should act justly. An appreciation of true justice derives from wisdom.

Maat Temple

As for the neteru associated with the previous degrees, create an inner temple of Maat and ask for her to inhabit it. The temple of Maat should be a place of light. Within its walls are no shadows or hidden areas. Maat is about what is not hidden, but does also incorporate the concept of silence. This is the silence of peace, of a quiet heart, the contemplative silence. As you create your temple, make sure the colour blue and the symbol of the ostrich feather, associated with Maat, are prevalent.

In this environment of light and quiet, you can escape the constant noise of mundane reality. When you visit the temple of Maat, do so in silence. Do not play music and do as much as you can to eliminate outside sounds. Reflect upon the idea that within this quiet you can communicate with your inner self more easily. The small voices of your being can be heard.

Ashash-t Work

When working on Ashash-t, begin by enlivening the other shefats, starting with Sen-t. The energy vitalises the red shefat of survival, rising through the orange of desire and creativity, through the golden yellow of projected will into the green heart centre of Ab. The energy then rises into the throat and Ashash-t, the seat of truth and communication. Visualise the brilliant blue of this shefat. Feed it with the energy of Sekhem Heka and see it begin to spin.

As Ab tempers the energy of Hati and projected will, so the light of truth and honest communication enhances and purifies our experiences. Ashash-t helps us discern what is truth and what is delusion, what is wishful thinking and 'what is'. We may have the power to change our reality, but first we must be able to view that reality objectively, not coloured too strongly by what we want to believe or what we fear might be so. As you meditate upon the issues that concern you, chant softly *em un maat*, which means 'this is really so'. Ask Maat for truth to be shown to you. But remember there are many truths; what is true for you might not be true for another.

We might regularly bite back our words and seethe quietly over situations, because we fear the consequences of speaking honestly. Repressed energy can build in Ashash-t, eventually blocking this shefat, which we can release through working on it.

Tu-Nut Initiation and Attunement

The student should sit comfortably with their hands in the Tui posture. You summon the shining light of Sekhem Heka, by drawing Tcheru, Tcher-Sekhem and Tchet-it symbols in the air and visualising the ray streaming down from the cosmos. Raise your hands above your head and then sweep them down. This gesture is to bring the light down to earth.

The following is the opening statement of intent. You can use my version or adapt it to your preference:

I call upon the mysterious ray of Sekhem Heka, in all of its power and brilliance. I call upon the adepts of the Ancient Egyptian mystery schools, to be present here and bestow their blessings upon these proceedings. I call upon the gods and goddesses of Ancient Khem, and to any guides or guardians who have a connection with those here present, to join us now, and bestow their blessings, upon Tu-Nut, this fifth degree Sekhem Heka initiation.

Say to the student:

Visualise that you find yourself in the Temple of Maat. You stand before a statue of Maat. We will call to her and awaken her.

Recite:

Oh Maat, Daughter of Ra,
Consort of Thoth
Personification of Order, Law and Truth
Lady of Heaven, Queen of the Earth
And Mistress of the Underworld

We come before you to walk in the light of truth, the Way of Maat
May your light banish all deceit, delusion and falsehood
May our words be just and powerful
May we always act honourably and may our decisions be wise
Guide our footsteps upon the Way of Maat
Lady of the Plume,
Goddess of cosmic harmony.

Tell the student:

You see a brilliant light emerge from the ankh in Maat's hand, which indicates she has heard us. Her statue comes alive. She gazes into your eyes and her expression is full of understanding. She sees right into you, to your true self.

Now perform the attunement.

As before, simply adapt your usual attunement procedure, but incorporate the symbols Tcher-Sekhem, Tcheru and Tchet-it. If you wish, you could include the Maat glyph of the feather, or else perform a separate attunement to Maat energy. A full version of a suggested attunement set is given in the appendices.

When attuning the crown, visualise that you push these symbols down into the brain stem along with the Usui ones.

When drawing the Cho Ku Rei on the palms of the hands, and 'slapping' them in, include Tcheru and Tchet-it also.

After the attunement, resume the visualisation.

Visualise Maat coming towards you. Be aware of her power, and how it is mirrored within you. Maat holds out her hands to you, and above them dances a star.

See the Tchet-it symbol come out of the star and enter your body at the Ashash-t shefat.

Thank Maat for the symbol, and spend a few moments communing with her. She may have important things to tell you or want to give you a symbolic gift.

After a few minutes, call the student back from their meditation and end the session. Affirm that the initiation is complete.

Khesu Tep Ra

Tep Ra is a term for 'mouth' so literally this is the rite of mouths. This rite is designed for those who wish to use the power of 'word of mouth' to help them in their lives. It especially applies to creative people or those in business who wish to enlarge their sphere of influence. The more people who know and talk about what you do, the more success comes to you. You can also perform this rite for other people.

Create your ritual space in your usual way and call upon the power of Sekhem Heka to flow through you and empower your working.

Visualise the Tchet-It symbol before you and enliven your Ashasht shefat by seeing it begin to glow blue. Draw the Tchet-It symbol towards you, into the shefat.

Now visualise a web of blue lines of light emanating from your Ashasht shefat. The lines criss-cross and curve. Wherever they cross is a brighter node of light, which represents another person.

Imagine that your ideas, your creative endeavours, or whatever you wish to promote, run as an essence along the lines of light, reaching all of the nodes. Visualise the network expanding ever outwards and your intention continuing to flow through it.

Also visualise whoever sees or hears about your work talking to other people about it, and that those people also pass the idea along to many others. Thus the spreading network is created.

When you are ready, conclude the rite as you normally would.

The imagery in this meditation is also a good metaphor for the Internet, which is the best network of communication we have at our disposal today. If you use the World Wide Web to promote your work or your creativity, you can incorporate this imagery into your rite, imagining the Internet as the vast spreading web of light, with the concentrated nodes representing others accessing that web.

Khesu Khnemes S-Netchem
(*kher*-nem-ess ess-*netch*-em)

Khnemes is a word meaning friendship, to behave as a friend or to be on good terms with someone, while S-Netchem means to make pleasant or happy or to heal. This is the rite of healing rifts in relationships – something we all have to deal with at one time or another. You can perform this rite for yourself or for someone else.

One of the main components in relationship upsets – whether within the family, at work, between lovers, or in a social group - is misunderstanding and assumption, based on lack of communication. Quite often, rifts happen because one or both sides of an argument stubbornly turn their backs and refuse to communicate. It might be that other people's words sway someone close to you to create a division, and the person concerned refuses to hear your side of the story. Over time, this cements the situation into one that is hard to remedy.

This khesu is designed to bring the light of Maat, of truth and harmony, to a situation in order to heal it. It can be performed soon after a rift has occurred but you can also use it to heal situations that might have happened years ago. Think carefully though about how much you want to resurrect from the past, both in terms of what is good for you and for others. Some situations it's best to let lie and put down to experience. If in doubt, meditate upon Maat and her symbol, the feather, for guidance, but listen honestly to what your instincts want to tell you.

It might seem to you that asking for everyone involved in a fiery fallout to suddenly become reasonable and open to communication with their perceived enemies is a really tall order. Therefore, perform this rite as you would a sutcha;

simply let go, put aside doubts that it can have effect, and trust in the energy to do its work. Have no attachment to any outcome of the rite.

Create your ritual space as you normally do and call upon Sekhem Heka to flow through you and to empower your working.

Compose yourself for meditation and enter your inner temple of Maat. See a statue of the goddess before you. She is depicted as kneeling on one knee, her arms outstretched. Concentrate upon the feather in her head-dress, as this represents truth and order.

Say:

Oh Maat, Daughter of the Cosmos,
Lady of Harmony,
I ask now that your bring your powers of truth
To bear upon this situation.
Awaken to me and hear me now.

See the statue come alive before you, the feather of Maat beaming out a powerful light. Say to the goddess (you can adapt these words according to what is appropriate for your situation, and even insert individual names for people involved in it.):

Oh Maat,
Let all who are in misunderstanding understand
Let all those who speak untruth be revealed for what they are
Let those who are hurt listen
Let those who have hurt them listen
Let those who will not speak begin to speak
Let feelings be expressed in truth and not judged.

For those who have turned their backs in haste and anger,
Let them turn again.
For those who have run in fear, let them turn back in courage.
Let all involved appreciate and respect the views of others.
Through your light and power,
May communication and harmony be restored.

If you wish to, describe in detail the situation to Maat. It's important you express these words aloud, no matter how strange you might feel doing so.

Finally, visualise the feather of Maat and the Tchet-It symbol in blue light and beam them towards the object of your working, the people involved. If you are attuned to a healing system, you can use a sending symbol to augment this part of the rite.

Visualise that all concerned are communicating again, and in honesty. See that the communication takes place in temperance, without anger, and that everyone involved is prepared to listen to what others have to say without losing their temper or taking things personally. Simply imagine that the light of Maat and Sekhem Heka soothes a volatile situation, so that suddenly everyone, even people who might not ordinarily do so, act with tolerance, understanding and compassion. Visualise that the situation is resolved.

When you are ready to conclude the khesu, thank Maat for her assistance and see her become once more a statue of stone. Then return to normal consciousness.

Khesu Maati
A Rite of Self Honesty
(*mah*-tee)

When looking at our lives and attempting to improve them, we also need to look at ourselves with utter clarity. All too often, we have warped ideas about ourselves, either too negative or too positive.

Sometimes you might put yourself down unnecessarily and have no faith in your skills or abilities, when really you are rather good at something, while at another time you might have overblown fancies about how good at something you actually are.

The trick is to find a fine balance; to look at ourselves honestly and perceive our own strengths and weaknesses – again without judgement.

For this meditation, compose yourself as you normally would within your ritual space.

Call upon Maat, visualising her feather and the Tchet-It, and ask for truth and clarity.

See yourself through Maat's eyes. Examine your situations, dilemmas, quandaries and relationships. All too often in life, all we have to go on is assumption about how others see us. Relax into the meditation and, remembering not to judge, analyse or criticise what might come to you, observe your situation. Imagine that the veils of delusion and confusion melt away.

Tu-Nut Healing Session

When working upon Ashash-t, begin by progressing through the lower shefats as previously described.

This healing can concentrate on matters of self expression, communication, the ability to listen to others, and honest self awareness. It can be focussed upon creative blocks, if necessary, or to help creative individuals find the ideas and inspiration they need.

Sas-Nu
The Sixth Degree

Wadjet was a goddess of the north, and in some forms of modern Egyptian magical ritual is visualised standing in this quarter. But primarily she is the goddess of the uraeus, the serpent that adorned the front of the crowns of kings and queen in Ancient Egypt. It might be more accurate to say that she *is* the uraeus, in full cobra form. The uraeus itself can be seen as a symbol of the third eye, which is said to reside in the centre of the forehead. It also represented wisdom and knowledge.

The third eye is believed to allow us to gaze upon that which is not perceived by the ordinary senses. Some writers on the subject now believe that the pituitary gland might well be this legendary organ, perhaps having atrophied from an earlier time of human development or yet to come into its own as we evolve as a species. In Sekhem Heka, the uraeus fits neatly into the sixth shefat, which equates to the third eye.

Wadjet was sometimes depicted as having a lioness's head, similar in appearance to Sekhmet, and she would usually have a uraeus in front of the solar disk upon her head. In other forms, she could appear as a snake with a woman's head or a snake-headed woman, but she could also be shown in full human female form, wearing the tall crown of the north, of which she was the patron goddess. In the northern Delta area, she had a cult centre at Per-Wadjet, which the Greeks called Buto.

The word 'wadjet' has several meanings but one of them signifies blue and/or green. One of the goddess's titles is 'The Green One'. It is also another form of the word Utchat, which refers to one of the eyes of Horus. The right eye symbolised the sun, and the left eye the moon. Wadjet is associated with the moon eye, which represents insight and magical wisdom. Her association with eyes goes further, as she was also one of the Eyes of Ra, who were sent forth to smite the sun god's enemies. The symbol for this degree is Ma-Her, the flash of lightning that emanates from the Eye of Horus.

Another of Wadjet's correspondences is to the Milky Way. This was seen as a great cosmic serpent, whose body was comprised of the spiralling stars of the galaxy.

The aim of this degree is to expand and strengthen inner sight, but it is also about intuition. Our inner selves are far more capable than our conscious selves of interpreting information around us. We all get 'gut feelings' from time to time, which might seem to contradict the evidence before us. Instincts are called 'animal instincts' because they are part of our natural self preservation abilities. Being able to sense things in this way gives us more information upon which to act.

As well as expanding inner sight and honing instincts, Sas-Nu is as much concerned with 'paying attention'. There is so much information around us and sometimes we ignore the details, skimming over the obvious. Our instincts and inner sight can assist us in reading others. A person might behave one way, but your guts might sense it's a front to conceal their real feelings or possible action.

The 'flight or fight' animal instinct belongs in the base shefat, along with others that are associated with pure survival. The instincts of Aar-t are more concerned with assessing situations and people.

Other aspects of Sas-Nu are imagination and dreams. This is the realm of creativity, visualisation and art. Our creative endeavours spring from our capacity to visualise and imagine. Writers, artists and musicians will have well developed sixth shefats.

As Aar-t is associated with imagination, so the whole concept of how we see ourselves – our body image – is associated with this shefat.

If the sixth shefat is deficient, the person concerned is likely to lack sensitivity and imagination. They are trapped in the mundane world, most likely scornful of any concept of 'sixth sense'. They are unlikely to be able to remember their dreams, and some might even say they don't dream at all. This is actually unlikely; they just don't have recall of them. If such individuals do begin magical training, as part of awakening this shefat, it's likely they will have a lot of difficulty with learning to visualise.

An over-active Aart-t can give rise to the person who suffers from delusions and who can't easily differentiate between fantasy and reality. They will probably be able to recall their dreams in intimate detail, and quite often those dreams can be terrible. The imagination is on over-drive, dominating the personality with no recourse to grounding. In extreme cases, it can lead to hallucinations.

When Aart-t is healthy and balanced, it leads to a balanced and perceptive person, whose intuition is keen, and whose dream recall is efficient. They will be imaginative and visionary without being delusional, and usually adept at visualising. Those who are naturally psychics have fully-functioning third eye shefats.

The Aui of Sas-Nu - Antch

The hand position for this degree is Antch – which means 'the tip of a wing', and also 'light, radiance, splendour'.

The hands are held up before the face in the Tui posture, with the thumbs resting against the bridge of the nose.

Slightly open the palms so that you can see through your hands. Imagine the Sekhem Heka ray streaming from your palms. Between them is a gateway to the multiverse, created by the flow.

Now, visualise your consciousness going into that gateway. Then see yourself passing beyond the gateway onto a highway of light. This can be visualised as the spiral arm of our galaxy, the Milky Way.

Use this aui when practicing the symbol meditations below. You can also use it when you wish to gather information about a situation or a person. Use the symbol and the highway of light to focus upon that which you wish to explore.

Meditation Upon the Ma-Her Symbol

Ma-Her Meditation for the Attuned

Compose yourself for meditation and connect with Sekhem Heka energy through the Tcheru.

Clear your mind and then visualise the Ma-her symbol shining before you. Spend some time gazing inwardly upon it, and see what ideas come to you concerning its use for you personally, or any personal meanings for it.

Place your hands over your third eye shefat for a self healing and keep visualising Ma-Her. It is used to expand your perception, hone your intuition and inspire your creativity. Imagine that the deep indigo radiance of this symbol fills your being. In the light of this radiance, energy that might have become trapped within the shefat, resulting in confusion, an inability to read events or people using your 'sixth sense', or creative blocks, is released.

Concentrate also upon how you see yourself; is your self image based upon reality or illusion? We all tend to think negatively about ourselves. Are your views correct or based upon ideals about what you should or should not be in a physical sense? Contemplate that if you imagine yourself, you can change that image.

Experiment with using the Ma-her symbol in conjunction with the Usui sending symbol, or if you have not reached second degree, simply by connecting with the energy and using the symbol as you 'beam' it.

Ma-Her Meditation for the Non-Attuned

Compose yourself for meditation and connect with Sekhem Heka energy through the Tcheru.

Clear your mind and then visualise the Ma-Her symbol shining before you. Spend some time gazing inwardly upon it, and see what ideas come to you concerning its use for you personally, or any personal meanings for it.

Draw the symbol in the air before you and say its name three times. As you do so, intend this symbol to represent your power 'to know'. It is the clear sight that allows you to access the inner realms, where your instinctive self is able to interpret signs and symbols in the environment, the body language of others. Visualise that any energy that has become blocked and trapped in the Aar-t shefat, is now released.

Move your focus over to your own body. Contemplate your body image, how you 'imagine' yourself. How true is this image? Consider the idea that what you imagine becomes your reality. Therefore, it is possible to reimagine yourself.

Meditate for some minutes upon having the ability 'to see and to know'. Your inner sight is capable of picking up much more information than your conscious self. It is this that you can access by enlivening the Aar-t shefat.

Communing with Wadjet

In Sekhem Heka, Wadjet represents the sight of the 'third eye', the inner sight of mystical knowledge. As with the 'gut instincts' associated with Sent-t, we are often taught or encouraged to ignore our intuition and to operate only on empirical evidence and 'facts'. However, whether you regard the sight of the third eye as a mystical, magical faculty or not, there is no doubt that our minds and senses pick up signals from the environment constantly, often at a subliminal level, which if we can access them enable us to have a wider picture of reality and the people within it.

Working upon Aar-t, enables us to see with 'clear sight'. This is the gift that Wadjet can bestow. In order to be fully functioning beings, we need to be aware, free of delusion. Working up through the shefats enables us to 'clear the way' to the higher shefats of Sas-Nu and Sefekh-Nu.

Wadjet Temple

 Wadjet's main cult centre was at Per-Wadjet, later known as Buto. Its remains still exist to this day at Tell el-Farein, near to Alexandria in the Delta. But the etheric temple of Wadjet should properly be a palace of dreams and imagination. When you build the temple in visualisation, incorporate into it symbols that represent these qualities to you. The sixth shefat is associated with the sense of sight and light. The temple of Wadjet can be lit by bright starlight, the light of a million suns.

If you wish, you could approach your temple

through the stars of the Milky Way. The symbol of Wadjet is the cobra, which is part of the hieroglyph of her name. Include within the temple imagery of serpents and decorative eyes. In its inner sanctum, where the goddess should be invited to reside, your imaginative intuitive self is released and nourished.

Visit the Temple of Wadjet to gain insight into situations and people and also to seek assistance with creative projects. As you create your temple, establish that when you go there ideas will come pouring to you. It is your creative sanctuary.

You can also visit the temple to interpret dreams and to meditate upon images you receive in visualisation. Again, intend that the temple enables you to gain clarity and insight into symbols that perplex you.

Aar-t Work

When working on Aar-t, begin by enlivening the other shefats, starting with Sen-t. The energy vitalises the red shefat of survival, rising through the orange of desire and creativity, through the golden yellow of projected will into the green heart centre of Ab. The energy then rises into the throat and Ashash-t; the seat of truth and communication. From here, it rises into Aar-t. Truth is enhanced by insight. Visualise the deep indigo light of this shefat. Feed it with the energy of Sekhem Heka and see it begin to spin.

Working upon Aar-t awakens latent psychic abilities, and sharpens the senses. It also nourishes creativity.

One of the most important functions of a healthy Aar-t is having discernment about what is real and what is not. If we exist wholly in the realm of dreams it's easy to become lost in them. We need to be able to discriminate between illusion and reality. Work upon Aar-t to achieve this objective and clear sight of the self.

Another aspect of working with this shefat is attuning yourself to the significance of signs and symbols around you in everyday life. Ancient seers and witches would be constantly aware of omens in their environment and pay attention to the messages they found there. If you are awake and alive in the world, paying attention to the details around you, so these signs will become more apparent and visible.

You have worked through all the lower shefats and now enter the realms of the cosmos, the higher spheres. Aar-t is the penultimate centre before the seventh; it is the gateway to the stars.

Sas-Nu Initiation and Attunement

As with the previous attunements/initiations, you can include your own sacred space creating practices if you want to. Alternatively, use the Utchat and the Ankh to create a Sekhem Heka temple.

The student should sit comfortably with their hands in the Tui posture. You summon the shining light of Sekhem Heka, by drawing Tcheru, Tcher-Sekhem and Ma-Her symbols in the air and visualising the ray streaming down from the cosmos. Raise your hands above your head and then sweep them down. This gesture is to bring the light down to earth.

The following is the opening statement of intent. You can use my version or adapt it to your preference:

I call upon the mysterious ray of Sekhem Heka, in all of its power and brilliance. I call upon the adepts of the Ancient Egyptian mystery schools, to be present here and bestow their blessings upon these proceedings. I call upon the gods and goddesses of Ancient Khem, and to any guides or guardians who have a connection with those here present, to join us now, and bestow their blessings, upon Sas-Nu, this sixth degree Sekhem Heka initiation.

Say to the student:

Visualise that you find yourself in the Temple of Wadjet. You stand before a statue of the goddess. We will call to her and awaken her.

Recite:

Oh Wadjet,
Eye of Ra,
Green One
Protector of Horus,
Lady of the Fiery Eye,
Bring to us the illuminating violet fire of the lunar
eye.
Empower our inner sight
Let us see beyond the mundane world
Let our instincts be true guides upon the path of
life
That we may see with the Eye of Heru, wider than
the sky.

Tell the student:

You see a brilliant light emerge from Wadjet,
which indicates she has heard us. Her statue
comes alive. She gazes into your eyes and her
expression is full of understanding.

Now perform the attunement.

As before, simply adapt your usual attunement
procedure, but incorporate the symbols Tcher-Sekhem,
Tcheru and Ma-Her. If you wish, you could include the
Wadjet glyph, or else perform a separate attunement to
Wadjet energy.

When attuning the crown, visualise that you push these
symbols down into the brain stem along with the Usui
ones.

When drawing the Cho Ku Rei on the palms of the

hands, and 'slapping' them in, include Tcheru and Ma-
her also.

After the attunement, resume the visualisation.

> Visualise Wadjet coming towards you. Be aware of
> her power, and how it is mirrored within you. She
> holds out her hands to you, and above them
> dances a star.
> See the Ma-Her symbol come out of the star
> and enter your body at the Aar-t shefat.
> Thank Wadjet for the symbol, and spend a few
> moments communing with her. She may have
> important things to tell you or want to give you a
> symbolic gift.

After a few minutes, call the student back from their
meditation and end the session. Affirm that the initiation
is complete.

Khesu Ar-t Tchef-t
(Aahtay Tcheftee)

Ar-t is sight, and Tchef-t is a word for serpent. Therefore this khesu is literally a ritual of the serpent of sight. It is a small rite designed to help with the opening of Aar-t.

Close your eyes and compose yourself for meditation. Concentrate upon the darkness before your mind's eye. Spend a few moments gazing inwardly upon it and note any colours or images that appear to you.

Now slowly will that the darkness becomes complete. Shift your focus to inside your head. Visualise the 'third eye' as a sleeping serpent of a brilliant emerald green colour, dappled with deep indigo markings. This serpent is a representation of Wadjet, who is a symbol for the clear sight of the sixth shefat.

Say:

> 'Wadjet, Lady of the Fiery Eye
> The Green One,
> Awaken within me the true sight of the serpent.
> Help me to behold that which is unseen,
> And to see through the veils of delusion
> Let us become one, Oh Wadjet
> Guide me along the path of the Cosmic Serpent
> To the stars.'

Concentrate upon drawing the energy of Sekhem Heka into Aar-t, and as you do so, it vitalises the serpent.

Visualise now that the serpent begins to stir. It lifts its head, and its eyes are bright jewels emitting an indigo light. The serpent uncoils and stretches itself. Like a vapour, it pushes through your forehead and pauses there, swaying. Imagine now that the serpent is like the uraeus on the crown of a pharaoh. It emerges from you like a jewelled diadem.

Focus upon seeing through the eyes of Wadjet's serpent; it is a part of yourself. It's a part that has been sleeping or semi-dormant. Meditate for some minutes upon having the serpent sight.

Khesu Resut

(rez-*oot*)

Resut is an Ancient Egyptian word for dreams. Dreams are our link to our subconscious minds. In our sleep, we live in an alternate universe where there is no logic, and the laws of the mundane world do not apply. Signs and symbols are the language of the dreamscape and we can learn much from them.

People with highly developed Aar-t shefats have good dream recall, while others, who lack this development, might say they remember absolutely nothing about their dreams. This is something that everyone can work upon.

Before you go to sleep, it's important to have the intention to dream with meaning. If you feel it will assist you symbolically, draw a representation of the Wadjet serpent upon your forehead before going to bed, and/or sleep with a drawing of the symbol beneath your pillow. These acts empower your intention.

Breathe deeply, in through the nose and out through the mouth, to induce an altered state of consciousness. Visualise yourself standing before a mighty pyramid at night. The sky above you is encrusted with stars and you can see the serpent band of the Milky Way coiling across the heavens. Visualise that the tail of the serpent almost touches the peak of the pyramid.

Now climb up the pyramid. With each step imagine that you are drawing closer to the realm of dreams. As you climb, ask Wadjet to guide your footsteps in the dreamscape. Tell her you wish to have a dream of significance and to remember it. As you ask her these things, you realise she is now walking beside you. Her footsteps leave a trail of light.

At the top of the pyramid, you see that the serpent of stars is a road of light. With Wadjet beside you, walk upon this road, into the realm of dreams.

If you do not fall asleep while doing this, or other thoughts begin to intrude, just let your mind wander as it wills. You have made your statement of intent and acted upon it. Trust that your dreams will be vivid and you will remember them.

When you awake, write down anything that you can remember. Sometimes the messages you receive will be obvious, but other time you might need to think about them for some time, or meditate upon the symbols to interpret their meaning.

Sas-Nu Healing Session

Use the Ma-her symbol upon yourself and others in a healing session. You can use this to work upon psychic abilities or the enhancement of insight and intuition. It is also associated with finding creative inspiration.

Intend for the symbol to strengthen your inner sight and instincts. This symbol can also be used to open and heal the Aar-t shefat. It might be that you, or someone you are healing, suffer from an inability to judge situations correctly, resulting in confusion and therefore an inability to act. Working with Aar-t and Ma-her helps instil the clarity needed to judge situations objectively.

If someone is troubled by dreams, it would also be appropriate to concentrate healing in this area, asking Wadjet to help the person concerned to interpret what their subconscious minds are trying to show them.

Sefekh-Nu
The Seventh or Tchaas Degree

Sefekh-Nu is what is known as the Master degree in other systems. In Sekhem-Heka, it is known as the Tchaas degree. Tchaas in Ancient Egyptian had several meanings. As well as being the title of a master and commander, it meant to command, to know, to have knowledge, and the wisdom of ancient times. It seemed an appropriate term for this level of Sekhem Heka.

A Master or Teacher of Sekhem-Heka is Shesa-t (*shess*-at) for women, which means 'wise woman' and Tchaasu (*char*-soo) for men, which means 'wise man'. I used these terms to denote individuals who have worked through the system, thereby having knowledge and 'mastery' of it. The wisdom here refers to the possession of knowledge of the system – not necessarily that those people are 'wise' in the ordinary sense. These are terms you can use if you wish to teach Sekhem-Heka.

The neter associated with Sefekh-Nu is Nut, or Nuit. She was the daughter of Tefnut and Shu, and was seen as a goddess of the night sky. Her brother, Geb, was the earth. Nut is generally depicted as clothed only in stars, or else naked and her body comprised of stars. She can be visualised as spiritual connection with the divine. She bestows understanding, knowing and spiritual bliss and conveys messages from the higher realms.

The shefat of this degree is Qemhu, the crown, which is seen as the seat of the higher self. It relates to the pineal gland, which along with the pituitary gland, associated with the sixth shefat, is connected with extra-sensory perception.

There are two symbols for this degree, which can be regarded as the 'Master' symbols. These are the Tcher-Sekhem and the Aakhu.

Having worked our way up through the shefats, so a gradual blossoming of the centres has occurred. Sefekh-Nu represents true freedom. Once we are free of the ignorance and fear that has blocked us, once we can emerge, perhaps raw yet eager, from the shells we created for ourselves, and which stunted life, we can experience what liberation actually feels like. It does not come from outside; from possessions, status or relationships with others. It comes from within and it is our own spark of the sacred. Through Qemhu we are in contact with our essential divinity. It is our connection with what is beyond ourselves, whatever we visualise that as being.

Sefekh-Nu is experience of god/dess, or whatever you want to call it, but it is also the shefat of religion and spirituality in general, and like all the shefats can have its deficiencies and excesses. This can manifest as over devotion to a belief, a refusal to take in more information, which can lead to dogmatism, repression and intolerance of others' beliefs. This doesn't just include individuals who have aligned themselves with a restrictive or ascetic belief system, but also those who might have suffered because of being brought up in such a religion. For some, the idea of god/dess and religion represents denial, narrowness, guilt, shame and lack of joy, only to be regarded with disgust and distaste. Anything that smacks even faintly of religion is to be avoided and treated with scorn. But that is to deny what true spirituality is; an individual experience and connection, not subject to the rules and beliefs of others. It is not to deny the body in favour of the mind, or to seek to suppress natural impulses, as espoused by many organised religions. To be truly spiritual is to be on a permanent quest for knowledge, with an open, inquisitive mind, and not to be led down side paths where there are traps of belief from which it is difficult to escape. As the saying goes, 'belief is the death of intelligence'; therefore we should guard against entrenching ourselves in systems that curb the desire for knowledge and further experience.

Whatever belief systems we explore, they are but stepping stones. Some might be larger than others, perhaps like islands in the great rushing river of life, and we might pause there for longer to learn about them, but there are always other stones, other islands, and they wait only for us to encounter them. Once we have uncovered a stone, it is always there to be revisited. Imagine now the richness of this vast spreading network of inspirational places. It does not close up behind us, but simply grows ever larger.

For many, the desire to seek and to learn is wrapped up wholly in the views of others. Lacking confidence and self belief, it's easy to think that true knowledge lies only with those who claim to have it (and often charge to share it). But while life is full of teachers who cross our paths, our greatest teacher lies within. It is the quiet part of ourselves who watches all that we do and what happens to us. It is not bound up in opinion, judgement, fears and assumptions. This observer within sees far more than our conscious minds and it is the part of ourselves we seek to access during meditation and rituals.

Some people might see divinity as a god or goddess, while others might view it as a 'higher self', or else entities outside ourselves who are present to guide and advise us. Essentially, it does not matter which model you find most appealing and easiest to work with. As long as you have an open mind, and are prepared to allow your beliefs to be fluid, according to what new information you might receive, then your spirituality is healthy and nourishing.

In Sekhem Heka, we work with the idea that the Egyptian neteru are representative of divinity, but this system could be applied to any gods or goddesses who already exist or that you could dream into being.

Perhaps, near the conclusion of this work, a question we should be asking is how real these entities are. We can experience their presence physically, emotionally and spiritually during rituals; they can feel very real to the perceptions. But are there really animal headed entities floating around somewhere?

My personal view is that divinity itself is formless, or of a form beyond our limited human comprehension. It is the animating principle of the universe. In order to interact with it, over the millennia humans have devised masks and vehicles for this mysterious energy, and these are the countless gods and goddesses, spirits, elementals and angels, that we find in belief systems around the world. As people invest energy into these entities, through intention, will, belief and love, so they become more 'real' within the collective unconscious. I think that as people direct energy to such a being they shape and animate it, so that it gradually takes on a life of its own, fed by all that intention and devotion. Imagine just for a moment the thousands of souls across the world investing energy into a particular god or goddess. That's a big power source! So in one sense, yes I do think gods and goddesses are real, but in another I see them wholly as human creations. But that does not invalidate or denigrate them. They are avatars of something beyond our ability to perceive. We can manifest them in our lives and ask for their help along our path. We can develop personal relationships with them. But we should not make the mistake of falling into the trap whereby we submit all responsibility to these beings. They are not there to be worshipped and obeyed; that is not their function. They should be treated with respect, but their purpose is to help us evolve as individuals and as a species.

In these times, it might be difficult to see the human race progressing. All around us it appears ignorance, intolerance, selfishness, stupidity and fear are rising like a great black wave. But at the same time, people are quietly investigating new avenues of spirituality; something that was rare and secret, if not illegal, fifty years ago. For those of us who pursue this path, we should carry the light of hope and positivity. A kind thought does not seem as powerful as a gun, and in fact we might feel helpless because it often feels like there are far more guns than kind thoughts in the world, but all we can do is look after our own small corner of it and live to the best of our ability. It might seem small, and the task monumental, but the smallest efforts made against the rising tide must have an effect.

It's said that it's always darkest before the dawn, and humanity does indeed appear to be going through a very dark time. Quite often, in a magical sense, when such a dark time descends upon the individual magician, it presages a breakthrough, when a revelation occurs and a new level of being is reached.

While blind faith to a restrictive belief does nothing to advance us as individuals, sometimes we do have to have faith in the universe itself. We can view it as essentially benevolent or else as utterly indifferent. As we can shape our reality, can we perhaps not also shape the universe around us? If we are to believe in something, it is surely better to believe in goodness and hope rather than bleakness and hopelessness. Of course it might all be wrong, and there might be nothing higher than us and nothing beyond human life. The universe could just be a mechanical thing, or else entirely random and accidental. All of our thoughts and ideas about spirituality and universal energy could be a delusion designed to make life more bearable. But if we can affirm that possibility and still live in hope with the desire to become more evolved, then we are not wasting our time or kidding ourselves. The one thing we can trust in is ourselves and the reality that we shape in our daily lives.

If we can bring balance to Qemhu so we increase our intelligence and awareness, our ability to be inquisitive, open-minded and connected with the universe and others. Once Qemhu is awake and thriving, we have not found all the answers; we simply move onward, excitedly awaiting the next questions. This is the basis of true wisdom, true mastery.

The Aui of Sefekh-Nu - Sehetch
(seh-*hetch*)

The hand position for this degree is sehetch, which means 'heaven of stars'. In this position, your dominant hand reaches for the heavens, directing the universal energy, while the non dominant hand points towards the earth, grounding the energy.

You can use this posture at any time during khesus or attunements. It is good to use it at the beginning and ending of initiations. The sehetch posture is found in many traditions, from Buddhism to the Western Tradition of magic. It appears in most renditions of the Tarot card, The Magician (arcanum 1 of the major arcana). It is a traditional symbol of bringing divine power down to earth.

Meditation Upon the Sefekh-Nu Symbols

Tcher-Sekhem and Aakhu are the master symbols of Sekhem-Heka. The former represents the limitless heavens, while the latter represents the shining aakhu spirits, light raining down from the skies. If anything Aakhu *is* the ultimate symbol of the energy of Sekhem Heka. When being attuned to this symbol, intend that it will strengthen your ability to channel the energy, to communicate with your higher self and for your instincts and intuitions to be ever more accurate. The goddess of the stars sees everything, knows everything, arches over everything.

Tcher-Sekhem Meditation for the Attuned

Compose yourself for meditation and connect with Sekhem Heka energy through the Tcheru.

Clear your mind and then visualise the Tcher-Sekhem symbol shining before you. Spend some time gazing inwardly upon it, and see what ideas come to you concerning its use for you personally, or any personal meanings for it.

 Sit with your hands in a position most comfortable to you or that seems most appropriate. Keep visualising Tcher-Sekhem. Intend to use it to connect you with the divine, your higher self and the higher realms. Imagine that the deep violet radiance of this symbol fills your being. Let your imagination soar into the heart of the cosmos. Become one with the body of Nuit, the stars. In the centre, all is complete and important knowledge comes

to you.

Experiment with using the Tcher-Sekhem symbol in conjunction with the Usui sending symbol, or if you have not reached second degree, simply by connecting with the energy and using the symbol as you 'beam' it.[1]

Tcher-Sekhem Meditation for the Non-Attuned

Compose yourself for meditation and connect with Sekhem Heka energy through the Tcheru.

Clear your mind and then visualise the Tcher-Sekhem symbol shining before you. Spend some time gazing inwardly upon it, and see what ideas come to you concerning its use for you personally, or any personal meanings for it.

Draw the symbol in the air before you and say its name three times. As you do so, intend this symbol to represent your power 'to connect'. Visualise a journey to the heart of the cosmos, where the body of Nuit arcs over the heavens. Become one with her and the stars. Focus upon connecting with the divine and experiencing the bliss of this connection.

Meditate for some minutes upon having the ability 'to connect' with the divine. You are connected with all things that exist within the universe. Concentrate upon this idea; we are all connected. In the higher realms of bliss, we are free of all human fears and become divine ourselves.

Imagine yourself as a star.

Aakhu Symbol Meditation for the Attuned

Compose yourself for meditation and connect with Sekhem Heka energy through the Tcheru.

Clear your mind and then visualise the Aakhu symbol shining before you. Spend some time gazing inwardly upon it, and see what ideas come to you concerning its use for you personally, or any personal meanings for it.

Sit with your hands in the position that feels most appropriate to you and keep visualising Aakhu. Rays of light extend from the central circle, representing the knowledge of the heavens coming to earth. Meditating upon this symbol enables you not only to connect with this higher knowledge but to draw it down to you and absorb it. Let the light of Aakhu fill your being.

Experiment with using the Aakhu symbol in conjunction with the Usui sending symbol, or if you have not reached second degree, simply by connecting with the energy and using the symbol as you 'beam' it.

Aakhu Meditation for the Non-Attuned

Compose yourself for meditation and connect with Sekhem Heka energy through the Tcheru.

Clear your mind and then visualise the Aakhu symbol shining before you. Spend some time gazing inwardly upon it, and see what ideas come to you concerning its use for you personally, or any personal meanings for it.

Draw the symbol in the air before you and say its name three times. Contemplate how the symbol represents the knowledge of the heavens descending to earth. Imagine that you are showered in the rich violet rays of wisdom-giving light. You absorb that light, let it settle within you. Tcher-Sekhem connects you with the divine; Aakhu is the channel for divine knowledge to come to you.

Communing with Nuit

Nuit is the goddess of the sky, mother of Isis, Osiris, Horus the Elder, Set and Nephthys. Her body is the heavens, encrusted with stars. She was often depicted upon temple roofs, arching over all who walked beneath her. Usually, she is naked, but for the stars that cover her. Long held as a particularly mystical neter associated with the secrets of high magic, Nuit is the perfect embodiment of the seventh shefat: The symbol here is part of her name in hieroglyphs.

Qemhu, the sphere of the higher self, concerns transcendence, reaching a state where the body, mind and soul are in accord, past traumas are excised from our being, and we are free to contemplate the higher realms, no longer bogged down by the tyrannies of fear, shame, guilt, regret and ignorance. As has been said before in this book, this is an ongoing process and none of us can expect to achieve this desired state in only a short time, but that does not mean we cannot experience the bliss to be found in Qemhu. In Sefekh Nu we concentrate upon not only connecting with Nuit and what she represents, but *becoming* her.

In Nuit, you seek to affirm all the work you have done on the shefats. While you might not yet be the most enlightened being in the universe, you have embarked upon the path, shouldered responsibility for yourself and committed to working on issues that need to be resolved. It is now time not only to bask in the rapture of Qemhu, but also to venture back down through the shefats, bringing with you the knowledge and experience you gained on the way up. The idea is to integrate the whole being, not just strive for an elevated spiritual state. The first shefat, Sen-t, does not just represent the physical body and immediate physical needs but also the ability to manifest results. You can use its energy to ground that of the other shefats, bringing creative ideas into reality, dreams into being.

Nuit Temple

The temple of Nuit is the sky itself, the sky of an unpolluted world where the stars shine in abundance. Therefore, the temple you create in your inner world should either have no roof, or include a large area open to the sky. You could perhaps create it as a platform on a raised dais surrounded by columns, decorated with star motifs. There should be no representation of the goddess, other than her symbol inscribed upon the columns, but when you gaze up at the sky, you should be able to perceive the shape of her body there in the stars. As you stare at the sky, so the body of Nuit gradually comes into focus for you, appearing out of the constellations.

Visit this temple to merge with Nuit, the stars themselves. In this place you find true liberation, living solely in the moment. You are the god/goddess of the temple, Nuit's avatar. Imagine this as your wiser self, the observer inside brought out into the starlight.

Qemhu Work

When working on Qemhu, begin by enlivening the other shefats, starting with Sen-t. The energy vitalises the red shefat of survival, rising through the orange of desire and creativity, through the golden yellow of projected will into the green heart centre of Ab. The energy then rises into the blue throat centre, Ashash-t, the seat of truth and communication. From here, it ascends into the indigo light of Aar-t, and the inner sight of intuition, thereafter rising to above the head where Qemhu is situated. Visualise the vivid violet light of this shefat. Feed it with the energy of Sekhem Heka and see all of the shefats begin to spin.

Concentrate upon the energy rising upwards through all the shefats and experience what each shefat represents as you do so. In Qemhu lies the completed whole and the bridge to further experience and knowledge.

When meditating in Qemhu – and while focussing on this shefat you are *in* it – focus without strain upon surrendering desires and attachments to physical things and people. Simply *be* yourself, unfettered, full of potential and creativity. In this place, there are no demands put upon you. It is the realm of pure, liberated personal experience.

Once you have existed in this state for some minutes, noting all that you feel and perceive, gradually move your focus to connection with the divine. Experience your connectedness with all that exists, your part within the universal whole.

When you feel ready, visualise the energy of Qemhu beginning to cascade back down through the other shefats, bringing with it spiritual nourishment. Ground the energy in Sen-t.

Now visualise that the whole energy system is a constant cycle of movement, as energy travels up from Sen-t to Qemhu and back down again. Thus the grounding of Sen-t anchors the experience of Qemhu, and Qemhu inspires the mundane qualities of Sen-t. Each of the shefats is of equal importance, supporting each other. Focus upon each in turn and contemplate how they enliven and enrich each other.

Sefekh-Nu Initiation and Attunement

The student should sit comfortably with their hands in the Tui posture. You summon the shining light of Sekhem Heka, by drawing Tcheru, Tcher-Sekhem and Aakhu symbols in the air and visualising the ray streaming down from the cosmos. Raise your hands above your head and then sweep them down. This gesture is to bring the light down to earth.

The following is the opening statement of intent. You can use my version or adapt it to your preference:

> I call upon the mysterious ray of Sekhem Heka, in all of its power and brilliance. I call upon the adepts of the Ancient Egyptian mystery schools, to be present here and bestow their blessings upon these proceedings. I call upon the gods and goddesses of Ancient Khem, and to any guides or guardians who have a connection with those here present, to join us now, and bestow their blessings, upon Sefekh-Nu, this seventh degree Sekhem Heka initiation, the Tchaas degree, culmination of this course.

Say to the student:

> Visualise that you find yourself in the Temple of Nuit. The body of Nuit arcs over you.

Recite:

> 'Oh Nuit, whose body is the robe of the heavens,
> Shetayet, Mysterious One,
> Lady of the starry firmament
> May we merge as one.

Share with me the knowledge of the aeons
Free my being from unwanted fetters
Make me as starlight.'

Tell the student:

You see a brilliant light emerge from Nuit, which
indicates she has heard us. She gazes into your
eyes and her expression is full of understanding.

Now perform the attunement.

As before, simply adapt your usual attunement
procedure, but incorporate the symbols Tcher-Sekhem,
Tcheru and Aakhu. If you wish, you could include the
Nuit glyph, or else perform a separate attunement to
Nuit energy. A full version of a suggested attunement set
is given in the appendices.

When attuning the crown, visualise that you push these
symbols down into the brain stem along with the Usui
ones.

When drawing the Cho Ku Rei on the palms of the
hands, and 'slapping' them in, include Tcheru, Tcher-
Sekhem and Aakhu also.

After the attunement, resume the visualisation.

Visualise Nuit in the sky around you. Be aware of
her nature, and how it is mirrored within you.
From her body emerges a radiant star. See the
Tcher-Sekhem and the Aakhu symbols come out
of the star and enter your body at the Aar-t shefat.
Thank Nuit for the symbol, and spend a few
moments communing with her. She may have

important things to tell you or want to give you a symbolic gift.

After a few minutes, call the student back from their meditation and end the session. Affirm that the initiation is complete.

Khesu Sma Nuit

(*Seh*-mah *Noo*-it)

Sma means to unite or join with something or someone. In this khesu, you will merge with Nuit consciousness.

Compose yourself for meditation. You may wish to visit Nuit's temple to perform this rite.

Visualise the night sky above you, thick with stars. At first, as you gaze upon them, you can perceive no pattern within them, but then gradually an image comes into focus, that of the body of Nuit arching across the heavens.

Her hands and feet touch the earth, so that her being forms a cosmic gateway over you.

A path of light appears before you. Begin to walk up it beneath the arch of Nuit's body. As you walk, you become aware you are entering Nuit's actual being, a power that vibrates all around you.

At the top of the path stands a representation of the goddess in full female form. Gaze into her eyes. As you do so, starlight blazes out of them into your own eyes. Feel your connection with Nuit and gradually absorb her energy until you become one.

Now you possess the sight of Nuit and can perceive the heart of all things, all truths. Affirm to yourself that you are in control of your own destiny, that you are connected to every other living thing around you, part of a whole.

Spend some time meditating freely, going where your

imagination takes you.

When you feel ready to conclude the khesu, walk back down the path of light back into your own body. Re-establish your connection with mundane reality. Ground yourself by anchoring your being to the earth. Be aware of your breath, and move your fingers and toes. Before you open your eyes, contemplate how you are charged with the cosmic energy of Nuit.

Khesu Kheperu
(*kep*-er-roo)

Kheperu's meanings include manifestation, change, transformation, form and shape. This khesu is designed to help manifest dreams, thoughts and ideas into reality.

You can dress this khesu up by creating sacred space and calling upon Nuit, or you can simply meditate in your Temple of Nuit. The ritual trappings are not important. What matters are the intention and the force of will you put behind it.

Ideas are born in the upper shefats, and the faculty to express them lies in Ashash-t. But in order to achieve results, the energy needs to be brought down into manifestation.

Any magical working to affect reality is the process of visualising a desired result and then charging it with will and intention to aid its manifestation. The trick is to imagine what you want already exists, and if only for the short time of the working to *believe that fully*. This is often difficult for practitioners to achieve, programmed as people can be with doubt and negative expectations. You should clear your mind of all judgments and opinions as you perform this khesu. Exist in the moment and focus only upon the work in hand.

Write your desire upon a piece of paper, and surround it with symbols that will charge it with even more meaning and purpose for you. Keep the words direct and to the point.

Holding this in your hands, take yourself in visualisation to the Temple of Nuit. Activate all your shefats and see them spinning brightly. Now, walk the path of light to merge with the goddess and for some moments focus upon your own power.

Now imagine that the essence of your desire transforms into pure energy (you could visualise it as a symbol if you prefer), which rises up from what you wrote. Draw this energy into Qemhu. Hold it there and feed it with the violet light of the shefat. Now slowly draw that energy down through the other shefats, where it takes on the qualities and strength of each one. As it descends, focus upon how this is manifesting your desire in reality. You are already making it happen.

Ground the energy in Sen-t. Affirm that your desire manifests.

Spend no further time in meditation, but return to normal consciousness in the manner you usually do. Then forget about the working. It's best to immerse yourself in some physical activity.

Sefekh-Nu Healing Session

Use the Tcher-Sekhem and Aakhu symbols upon yourself and others in a healing session. Use this to work upon issues to do with spirituality, or lack thereof, and for people who are locked into their lower shefats. Use it to help yourself and others connect with universal intelligence and to bring the light of hope to areas of darkness and despair. It can be used to help people access their full potential.

Conclusion and Further Work

You have now reached the end of the seventh degree of Sekhem Heka. Now would be a good time to return to working upon the earlier shefats, noting how different the rituals and meditations feel to your earlier experiences.

The purpose of Sekhem Heka is to help you integrate all aspects of your being – earthly with heavenly, if you like – but not at the expense of the lower shefats. Our mundane lives are just as important as our spiritual lives; each should inform and nourish the other. Our work upon all the shefats should be continual and gradual.

The khesus of this system can be adapted for whatever purpose seems pertinent, or of course you can write your own khesus to expand your practice. Aakhu Sem upon you – the blessings of light. May your path be rewarding and true.

Appendix 1
Self Attunement

These attunement methods are primarily for Selchim/Reiki Teachers, but if you have taken second degree in any other system, you could still perform an adapted 'Attunement by Heka Khesu' (given below), for each degree, to help you 'lock on' to the symbols of Sekhem Heka. You do not have to be attuned to the symbols to work with them effectively.

You should not attune yourself to the Teacher degree unless you have received a similar attunement from a Teacher trained to that degree in one of the energy healing systems.

There are many methods to attune yourself, and all of them are equally effective. Some people simply visualise themselves and perform the attunement upon this visualised self; others use 'proxy' items such as soft toys to represent themselves; yet more use 'chi balls'.

In this system, I devised a self-attunement that involves calling upon Heka to come and perform the attunement upon you in visualisation. Some methods will be more suited to you than others. Choose the method that feels most comfortable and 'feels' right for you personally. Except for the visualisation of Heka method, the examples are adapted from common practices within the energy healing community.

Preparation

It is helpful to create a meaningful atmosphere for self-attunement. It is a rite of initiation even if you are taking part in it alone, without the company of a teacher or friends. Therefore, prepare your ritual space with some care, in respect of lighting, perfume in the form of burning oil or incense, and music. Take a bath beforehand, and prepare yourself in any other way you usually do for ritual work.

Before any of the methods given, begin with your statement of intent. Say aloud or in your mind (for example): 'I perform this ceremony to attune myself to the symbols and energy Sefekh-Nu, the Tchaas degree of Sekhem Heka.' If you so wish, you could elaborate upon this opening statement to include ideas, affirmations, goals and thoughts that are personal to you.

It would also be appropriate to call upon any guides, if you should work with them, and ask for them to augment the initiation.

Attunement from Heka

Connect with universal energy in your usual way. Breathe in the light of it and let it fill your being.

Connect with Sekhem Heka by visualising the two symbols and call upon the neter Heka to attune you. See him manifesting before you, and then visualise in detail him performing the attunement upon you. This might be in the manner you usually give attunements, or you might find that in the visualisation there is some change to your usual practice. Just allow the visualisation to flow.

Once it is done, Heka tells you that you have received the Teacher degree of Sekhem Heka and places his hands upon your shoulders to seal the attunement.

Sit for some minutes, allowing the energy to continue filling your being.

Chi Ball Attunement

Connect with the universal life energy, either as Reiki, Seichim, or whatever you have trained in.

Raise your arms high, with the palms of your hands upwards, and intend for the energy to come down from the centre of the universe and surround you.

Breathe in the energy as bright light, and direct it to the palms of your hands.

Lower your arms and bring your hands together, facing each other, about one inch apart.

While still focusing upon the energy entering and flowing through your body, slowly begin to move your hands apart. Visualise that a ball of energy forms between them.

Continue to move your hands until they are around 8 inches apart and a large ball of energy is visualised between them.

Now perform a Teacher attunement on the ball, by visualising the symbols going into it, along with the intent that this will attune you to Teacher level of Sekhem Heka. Use the symbols you normally use for attunement, and also all of the Sekhem Heka symbols.

To send the attunement to yourself, visualise the Hon Sha Ze Sho Nen symbol over the ball, drawing it in your mind from top to bottom of the ball.

State with your full will and intention that the attunement will be sent to yourself.

For a few minutes, sit quietly, with open mind, to accept the attunement from the Chi Ball.

State and intend that the attunement is now sealed and concluded.

Sit for as long as you wish, with hands in the Tui posture, and allow the energy to continue flowing through you.

Self Attunement by Proxy

With this method you can use any object that lends itself easily to representing you. This could be a soft toy, a picture of yourself, or even a cushion.

The method given here will use your own legs, specifically the thighs and the knees, to represent different parts of your body. It is probably better to use this method than, say, using a teddy bear to represent you, for the simple reason that in this method you work upon your own body.

The left thigh represents the front of your body, with the knee being your head.

The right thigh represents the back of your body, with the knee being the back of your head.

Place your hands upon the right knee, visualising that these are hands placed upon the back of your head. Establish a connection with the universal energy in your usual way.

Attune the head, using your usual attunement method, over your right knee, including the Sekhem Heka symbols. Intend that these symbols sink into the brain.

Place your hands in the tui posture before your Ab shefat and breathe in the Sekhem Heka energy.

Move your hands to the left knee and thigh, with the intention that you will now attune the front of the body.

Proceed with the visualised attunement as per your usual method.

To attune the hands, draw all the symbols on the palm of each hand intending that the attunement takes place. Slap them in, if that is your usual method.

Place your hands back upon the right knee, intending that the energy fills the crown.

Make any affirmations you wish. Allow the energy to pour in and use Hon Sha Ze Sho Nen to reinforce the attunement.

Seal the attunement with a closing statement.

Appendix II
Distance Attunement

Distance attunement is just as effective as an attunement given in person, and sometimes the energies received by the student can be experienced as even more powerful. Look upon it as the same as sending healing via the Hon Sha Ze Sho Nen symbol – as healing can be sent through time and space, so can attunements.

As with self attunement, several methods have been devised to send attunements over distance. Below are two examples:

Same Time, Different Place

This attunement is performed at the same time as the student is waiting to receive it. A mutually convenient time is established beforehand. Both Teacher and student prepare and compose themselves for the attunement, and should visualise that in the etheric realms, they are actually in the same space.

While the student sits with their hands in the Tui posture, the Teacher visualises and intends that the student is sitting before them. In the opening statement of intent, the Teacher should state that they are about to perform a distance attunement on the named student, and ask that the student receives the energies to the level they are able to receive.

Similarly, the student should make the same affirmation

and state aloud they are receiving the attunement from the named Teacher, and that they wish to receive the energies to the level they are able to receive.

The Teacher then performs the attunement, visualising that the student is there in person. They should simply perform their usual attunement set, incorporating the Sekhem Heka symbols where appropriate.

Different Time, Different Place

One of the benefits of a distant attunement is that a Teacher can prepare it in advance so that the student can 'call in' to receive it at a convenient time. This is helpful when a Teacher and student live in different countries, and time zones differ greatly.

As the Teacher prepares the attunement, they should intend and state how long it will remain available for 'collection'. They should also, as for the method above, state that the student should receive the energy to the level they can comfortably receive.

The attunement can be placed into a 'chi ball', which can then be stored in a visualised etheric 'bank'. The student can access their attunement simply by asking to receive it.

To create a chi ball attunement, call upon the energy you wish to work with, and focus upon creating a ball of it between your hands. Feed this ball with intention and let the energy flow from your palms.

When you feel the ball is ready, perform an attunement upon it as you would upon a person. If it helps you to focus, you could visualise a small version of your student sitting inside the ball to perform the attunement upon.

When complete, use the sending symbol to place the chi ball in your etheric 'bank'. Intend that it is there, waiting for the student to collect it, and then inform your student it is ready for them.

Appendix III
Sekhem Heka Attunement

This is a suggested attunement set for the seven degrees of Sekhem Heka. It is the full attunement method, minus certain aspects of the full khesus given in the previous sections.

Given below is an example attunement for Ha-a Degree. The attunement process is the same for all degrees, merely substituting the relevant symbol for each degree. For the Tchaas or Seventh Degree, put both Aakhu and Tcher-Sekhem into the palms.

If you prefer, you can simply adapt the attunement set you already use, incorporating the Sekhem Heka symbols where appropriate.

Prepare the room by creating a Sekhem Heka temple, using the appropriate symbols.

Student sits with hands in the Tui posture in front of you.

Draw Cho Ku Rei on your own palms, and also the Tcheru to connect with the universal energy and Sekhem Heka in particular.

Draw a large Dai Ko Myo in the air before you, almost as big as yourself, visualising it as the most brilliant light. Then draw the Tcher-Sekhem symbol in the same manner. Step into the symbols and absorb their merged energies.

Make your opening statement, calling upon the energy of Sekhem Heka, and intending that this is a first degree attunement for the named student.

Walk anticlockwise around the student to the back.

Perform Hui Yin if you wish – although this is not essential. You might have already been taught to pass attunements in this way. Flex the pelvic floor muscles while pressing the tongue against the roof of the mouth. This cultivates the cauldron of energy within the body so that crown and base shefats are completely connected.

Place hands upon the student's head for a while to make a connection with them. Then lift both hands off the student's head.

Put your non-dominant hand upon your hara (personal energy centre in the stomach). With dominant hand, draw Dai Ko Myo horizontally above the head, in the Qemhu shefat. Imagine it as purple light.

Draw Tcher-Sekhem and Cho Ku Rei in the same manner, then place your dominant hand back on the head.

Draw or visualise Hon Sha Ze Sho Nen in your mind, in purple. See your hand as transparent and direct the symbol down through it into the third eye shefat of the student.

Repeat with Sei He kei, Tcheru and Heka.

Visualise Dai Ko Myo and Tcher-Sekhem once more,

before your third eye.

Walk anticlockwise to front of student.

Briefly touch and steady the student's hands. Make sure they're in the right position, so you can blow over them at an angle onto the heart shefat.

Draw the 7 symbols above them: Dai Ko Myo, Tcher-Sekhem, Cho Ku Rei, Hon Sha Ze Sho Nen, Sei He Kei Tcheru and Heka.

Perform Hui Yin, holding the hands of the student, keeping your eyes closed.

Visualise the two master symbols, Dai Ko Myo and Tcher-Sekhem, again before your third eye, while holding your breath.

Open eyes and blow over student's fingers at an angle in the direction of the Ab shefat.

Raise hands of the student, so that their thumbs are about level with their forehead.

Repeat the symbols as before over the fingers.

Close eyes and visualise the two master symbols again, holding breath.

Open eyes and blow over student's fingers at an angle towards their third eye.

Now part student's hands and lower them, gently pressing the palms with your thumbs.

Draw the Tcheru and Heka over one palm and then

'slap' it.

Repeat with the other hand.

Place initiate's hands back together and raise them, so that their thumbs are pressed gently against their forehead.

Perform Hui Yin and visualise the Master symbols.

Blow across the top of the student's fingers across the top of the crown.

Lower student's hands and tell them that the attunement is now complete.

Sekhem Heka Attunement for Seichim/Sekhem/Reiki Teachers

You can perform an 'all in one' attunement on existing Teachers, by placing all of the Sekhem Heka symbols into the body at each stage of the attunement.

Appendix IV
Correspondences of the Degrees

First Degree

Name: Ha-a (haa-*ah*)
Shefat: Base, Sen-t (*sen*-tay)
Neteru: Heka and Sekhmet
Colour: Red
Symbols: Tcheru (infinity) (*cheh*-roo), Heka (hek-*aa*)
Aui: Tui (clean handed) (*too*-wee)

Second Degree

Name: Sen-nu (*sen*-noo)
Shefat: belly, Khep-ti (*kep*-tee)
Neter: Isis
Colour: Orange
Symbol: Tchem Aset (wings of Isis) (*chem*-az-*ett*)
Aui: Behut Aset (throne of Isis) (beh-*hut* az-*ett*)

Third Degree

Name: Khemt-tu (*kem*-too)
Shefat: solar plexus, Hati (*haa*-tee)
Neter: Ra
Colour: Yellow
Symbol: Aaten (sun disk) (*aah*-ten)
Aui: Temati (a pair of wings) (tem-*ah*-tee)

Fourth Degree

Name: Ftu-Nu (fuh-*too*-noo)
Shefat: heart, Ab
Neter: Bast
Colour Green
Symbol: Per-Ahu (per-*ah*-hoo)
Aui: Pesh-Ti (the two halves of heaven)

Fifth Degree

Name: Tu Nut
Shefat: throat, Ashash-t
Neter: Maat
Colour: Blue
Symbol: Tchet-it (the spoken word)
Aui: Uba Ab (to open the heart, to speak freely)

Sixth Degree

Name: Sas Nu
Shefat: third eye, Aar-t
Neter: Wadjet
Colour: Indigo
Symbol: Ma-her (the flash of light from Horus's eye)
Aui: Antch ('the tip of a wing' or 'light, radiance)

Seventh Degree

Name: Sefekh Nu
Shefat: crown Qemhu
Neter: Nuit
Colour: Violet
Symbols: Tcher-Sekhem, Aakhu
Aui: Sehetch (heaven of stars)

Glossary of Terms

Aakhu (*aah*-koo) – a symbol of the seventh degree, meaning 'shining'.

akhu - an Ancient Egyptian word for 'magical power'. It can also to apply to a spirit of the dead.

Aaten (*aah*-ten) – the solar disk, a symbol of the third degree.

Ab – the Egyptian word for heart, also the heart shefat (which see).

Amenti – the land of the Ancient Egyptian afterlife or interpretation of heaven.

Ankh – an Ancient Egyptian symbol meaning longevity and life itself.

Antch - The aui for the sixth degree, which means 'the tip of a wing', and also 'light, radiance, splendour'

Anubis – an Ancient Egyptian jackal-headed neter, associated with the cult of the dead.

Ar-t Tchef-t (*aah*-tay *tchef*-tee) A khesu of the sixth degree's sight, a ritual of the serpent of sight.

Aset (or Ast) (Az-*ett*) - the Ancient Egyptian name for the neter Isis.

Ashash-t (aah-*shash*-tay) – the throat or fifth shefat.

Au-ta (aw-taa) - An aui (which see), deriving from a word meaning to make an offering with open hands

Aui (*aw*-wee) – a term for the hand positions used in Sekhem Heka. Corresponds to mudra (which see).

Bast – a cat-headed female neter, associated with love, dancing, harmony.

Behut-Azet (beh-*hoot* Az-*ett*) an aui of the second degree, meaning 'throne of Isis'.

chakra – one of the energy centres of the body, from Asian spiritual belief.

Chi – life energy, universal energy, another word for 'ki'.

Cho Ku Rei (*cho*-koo-ray) – the power symbol of Reiki.

Dai Ko Myo (die-*koo*-mee-oh) – the master symbol of Reiki.

Ftu-Nu (fuh-*too*-noo – the fourth degree of Sekhem Heka.

gassho (*gas*-oh) – a mudra (which see) commonly used in prayer and meditation.

Ha-a (ha-*aah*) – the first degree of Sekhem Heka.

Hathor – a female neter associated with love, sometimes depicted with the head of a cow.

Hati (*haa*-tee) – the solar plexus or third shefat.

Heka – an Egyptian male neter, who personified magic.

heka – In Sekhem Heka, a term meaning 'chi' or 'ki', the universal energy. In Ancient Egypt, this meant magical power.

Hon Sha Ze She Non – the 'sending' symbol of Reiki.

Horus – a male falcon-headed neter, who is associated with the rising sun.

hu - Ra's divine utterances that helped bring about creation in Egyptian mythology.

Isis – a female neter, mother of Horus, wife of Osiris, strongly associated with magic.

Karuna Ki – a healing modality that derives from Reiki.

Khem – the ancient name for Egypt.

Khemt-tu (*kem*-too) – the third degree of Sekhem Heka.

Kheperu - manifestation, transformation, change, form and shape, a khesu of the seventh degree.

Khept-ti (*kep*-tee) – the belly or second sheft.

Khesu (*keh*-soo) – a rite or ritual.

Khnemes S-Netchem (*kher*-nem-ess ess-*netch*-em) – a rite of the fifth degree to heal rifts in relationships.

Khnum – an Ancient Egyptian ram-headed creator neter.

Ma-her (ma-*hur*) – a symbol of the sixth degree, which

means a flash of light from the Eye of Horus.

Maat – an Egyptian female neter associated with cosmic order, truth and harmony.

Maati (*mah*-tee) – a rite of the fifth degree, performed for self-honesty.

Ma-t (*mah*-tay) – a lioness, a Rite of Sekhmet, first degree.

Metu Terf (*meh*-too *turf*) – the principles of Sekhem Heka, which means 'words of wisdom'.

Aar-t (meh-*rit*) – the third eye or sixth shefat.

Mudra (*moo*-drah) – sacred hand positions and postures in Asian spirituality.

Naa – 'to sail away from' or 'to take pity on', part of the title of Khesu Naa, the rite of forgiveness.

neteru (*net*-er-roo) – the term for the gods and goddesses of Ancient Egypt, singular: neter.

Nekhnem (*nek*-nem) an Ancient Egyptian term for perfume.

Nuit (*noo*-it) – a female neter of the stars and sky.

Per-Ahu (*pair*-a-*hoo)* –a symbol of the fourth degree, meaning 'house of the heart'.

Pesh-ti (*pesh*-tee) The aui of the fourth degree, which means 'the two halves of heaven'.

Qemhu (*Kem*-oo) – the crown or seventh shefat.

Ra – a creator neter of Ancient Egypt, associated with the sun.

Re-Harakhte (*ray*-ha-*rak*-tee) – a form of Ra, combined with the falcon-headed Horus.

Reiki – an energy healing system founded by Mikao Usui in Japan, in the early 20th century.

Resut (rez-*oot*) – a words for dreams, a khesu of the sixth degree.

San Ab – a rite of the fourth degree, associated with perfume and healing of the heart.

Sas-Nu (*Saz*-noo) – the sixth degree of Sekhem Heka.

Sefekh-Nu (*sef*-ek-*noo*) – the seventh degree of Sekhem

Heka.

Sehetch (seh-*hetch*) The hand position for the seventh degree, which means 'heaven of stars'.

Sei He kei (zay-*heh*-kee) – the emotional/mental healing symbol of Reiki.

Seichim (say-*keem*) – an energy healing system founded by Patrick Zeigler in 1980, deriving from his own spiritual experiences and Reiki training.

Sekhem – an energy healing system deriving from Seichim.

Sekhem – an Ancient Egyptian word meaning 'power' or 'vigour'.

Sekhmet – a lioness-headed neter, associated with both healing and smiting.

Sen-nu (*Seh*-noo) – the second degree of Sekhem Heka.

Sen-t (*sen*-tay) – the base or first shefat.

Shef – the energy system of the body in Sekhem Heka; equates to chakras.

Shefat – the term to denote a single energy centre of the body.

Shesa-t (*shess*-at) – a term for female practitioners of Sekhem Heka who have completed all seven degrees, which means 'wise woman'.

sia – Ra's divine knowledge that helped bring about creation in Egyptian mythology.

SKHM – the current version of Patrick Zeigler's Seichim system.

Sma (*seh*-ma) – to unite with something or someone (Khesu Sma Nuit, a ritual of the seventh degree).

Sopdet – the Ancient Egyptian name for the star Sirius, in the constellation of Canis Major, near the constellation of Orion, seen as the birthplace of Isis.

Sutcha (*soo*-tcha) – a healing rite of the fourth degree designed to help overcome sadness/grief.

Tchaas - the seventh or 'master' degree of Sekhem Heka, meaning to command, to know, have knowledge.

Tchaasu (*char*-soo) – a term for male practitioners of Sekhem Heal who have completed all seven degrees, which means 'wise man'.

Tchem-Aset (*chem*-az-*ett*) – a symbol of the second degree, meaning 'wings of Isis'.

Tcher-Sekhem (*chair*-sek-*em*) – a symbol of the seventh degree, meaning 'limitless heavens'.

Tcheru (*cheh*-roo) – a symbol of the first degree, the infinity or lemniscate.

Tchet-it (*chet*-it) – a symbol of the fifth degree, meaning the spoken word.

Tchet-t (cher-tay) – the shefats of the palms of the hands.

Teb-ti (teb-tee) – the shefats of the soles of the feet.

Tehuti (teh-*hoo*-tee) – the Ancient Egyptian name for Thoth (which see).

Temati (tem-*ah*-tee) – an aui of the third degree, which means 'a pair of wings'.

Tep Ra – a rite of the fifth degree, performed to make use of the power of 'word of mouth'.

Thoth – an Egyptian neter of scribes, wisdom and knowledge.

Tu-Nut (*Too*-noot) – the fifth degree of Sekhem Heka.

Tui, (*too*-wee) – an aui associated with the first degree, which means 'clean-handed' or 'purified'.

Uba-Ab (*oo*-bah *ab*) The aui of the fifth degree, which means to open the heart, to speak freely.

Utchat – a symbol and a term meaning either eye of Horus.

Weret-Hekau (*weh*-ret hekk-*ow*) – a title of Isis, meaning 'great of magic'.

Bibliography and Resources

This is a short selection of recommended books and web sites.

Reiki

Maureen Kelly, Reiki and the Healing Buddha, Full Circle Publishing, 2003
Steve Murray, Reiki False Beliefs Exposed, Body and Mind Productions, 2006
Frank Arjava Petter, Reiki Fire, Motilal Banarsidass Publishers, 1998
Essential Reiki, Diane Stein, Crossing Press, 1995

Reikifire Ministry Symbol Library
http://reikispirit.net/church/sym.library.index.html
Useful resource for various energy healing symbols

Seichim

All Love, Patrick Zeigler's home page
http://www.all-love.com/members/alllove

A Short history of **Seichem/Seichim/Sekhem/SKHM All Love**
http://www.reiki-seichem.com/seichim.html

Chakras and Energy Healing

Anodea Judith, Eastern Body, Western Mind, Celestial Arts, 2004
John Mann and Lar Short, The Body of Light, Charles E Tuttle Inc, 1990
Diane Stein, Essential Energy Balancing, Crossing Press, 2000

Egyptian Studies

Storm Constantine and Eloise Coquio, Bast and Sekhmet: Eyes of Ra, Hale, 1999
Geraldine Pinch, Magic in Ancient Egypt, British Museum Press, 1994
Richard H Wilkinson, The Complete Gods and Goddesses of Ancient Egypt

Recommended Online Schools

Lady of the Flame Iseum – author's Iseum web site:
http://www.ladyoftheflame.co.uk
Lady of the Flame Iseum can provide attunements, should any practitioner prefer a more formal grounding in Sekhem Heka, basic training in Reiki and Seichim, or courses on various aspects of magic, including Egyptian. Certificates and manuals are provided. For more information, please contact info@ladyoftheflame.co.uk, with the email subject heading of 'Training Courses'.

The School of Living Reiki Therapies
http://www.livingreikitherapies.co.uk/
For those who do not have easy access to a Reiki/Seichim teacher, online distance courses are a viable alternative – as long as you are not overcharged for the service.

Jay Burrell, founder of The School of Living Reiki Therapies, has been the author's teacher for the most recent of her energy healing training. He offers a wide array of modalities, some quite exotic and intriguing, at an extremely reasonable price, with excellent post-training support. Jay is endorsed by the author to teach Sekhem Heka through his school.

Acknowledgements

I'd like to acknowedge all fellow travellers and teachers who've shared with me their knowledge, experience and expertise and who have all contributed to the creation of this work, either simply by being in my life and enriching my spiritual journey or else through hands-on assistance with Sekhem Heka itself.

My thanks to:

Andrew Collins who opened up new vistas for me magically and set me upon a starry road, and also for helping me shape the final tiers of this system; his wife, Sue Collins, for her support, friendship and magical times; Paul Weston for introducing me to healing energy and for the unforgettable and inspiring attunements; Caroline Wise, UK co-ordinator of the Fellowship of Isis, who also helped shape my path; Simon Beal, who worked with me on this system; Ellen Kesterton for her inspiring visionary work; Jay Burrell, my most recent energy healing teacher, for his generosity and expansive knowledge of many systems; Taylor Ellwood and Lupa for all their hard work and support; and last but far from least Patrick Zeigler who founded Seichim and without whose inspirations this work would not exist.

About the Author

Storm Constantine has been a Reiki/Seichim Teacher for eight years, and has studied magic and alternative spirituality for three decades. She is founder of the Lady of the Flame Iseum, a magical group affiliated to the Fellowship of Isis.

As a published author, she had produced over thirty novels and non fiction works. Most known in the fiction world for her ground-breaking Wraeththu novels, (all available through Immanion Press), she continues to weave her magical experience into her fiction.

Storm lives in the Midlands of England with her husband Jim and seven cats. As well as writing, she runs Immanion Press, and also teaches magical subjects, Reiki, Seichim and Sekhem Heka.

Lightning Source UK Ltd.
Milton Keynes UK
UKHW010918110321
380169UK00001B/200